Christian Reborn

The Breaking of the Final Chains

CHRISTINE RENEE

Faith, Hope, & Love Publishers

Christian Reborn
The Breaking of the Final Chains

First Printing, 2021

ISBN 978-1-7368772-0-3

Faith, Hope, & Love Publishers

Printed in the United States of America

Dedication

I would like to dedicate this book to all who are willing to take the journey of freedom to elevate their thoughts by coming into alignment with the will of the Trinity, which is the Father, Son, and Holy Ghost.

All honor to the one and only LORD who uses every opportunity to get us to the next level of our destination by any means necessary. To God be the glory for my journey.

Contents

Acknowledgments

I would like to acknowledge Jesus who is the Author and Finisher of my faith. The prayer warriors who have labored with me in prayer during the process of producing this book.

My daughters Eboni and Elexis. I have worked hard to make sure they have an aligned heart and mind, a legacy and a love that is unconditional in a personal relationship with Christ Jesus.

LYLAS Services is a nonprofit organization that provides accommodations for aged-out youth to a safe and loving home while offering edification, encouragement, and education. Proceeds from this book will be rendered to the funding of this organization in efforts to defeat child sex trafficking from the onset and keep our most vulnerable from being homeless once they are discharged from the foster care system.

The editor of this book, Oshin Hephzibah, was

a pure delight to work with. She executed major decisions, keeping in the flow and development of the writing style and subject matter while maintaining open lines of communication with the author throughout the process. Her professionalism, poise, and writing style was a beautiful addition to this work.

Preface

I am not who I used to be. Often times, we judge people based on the time in their lives we walk in on. We use the depth of these relationships to determine the role they play in our lives. We paint pictures of who we think they are and look for evidence to prove ourselves right in our assumptions of them. We rarely ever consider the source of change or their growth and development. And we never really stick around to witness the life-changing plans of God on their behalf.

It is true that we all sin and fall short of the glory of the Lord (Romans 3:23). However, I am here to introduce to some and reintroduce to others the opportunity of a saving grace that Jesus has provided for all of us sinners. If, in fact he did it for me, he will most definitely do it for you as well. Falling short has led many to understand

and acknowledge the true meaning of life. The love of Christ offers us all the opportunity to be free of sin.

I invite you to come sit in the dirt with me while I take you on a journey of my life, my heritage, my history of the slave mentality and how I truly found out that the love of God saves a wretched soul. There may be some unorthodox instances throughout the text that will force you to clutch your pearls. However, I assure you it will be fine if you allow yourself to just breathe through it. The concept will be made through a series of true stories.

Let me tell you a little about myself. I grew up in a Southern Baptist Church. When I was younger, the second Sunday service was routinely the time when we partook in communion. Sunday service was just something we did or so I thought. As I became an adult, I continued the routine as most Christians do. However, it took me moving away from my home state; to realize that there had to be something deeper than scratching the surface of the routinely church-going practices that I had been indulging in.

When I searched for more, I was led to a Holy

Ghost filled church on the West side of Detroit, MI. Greater Ebenezer Missionary Baptist Church based their belief on Southern Baptist principles. This was the start of something wonderful. I grew through this ministry and was content with the Genesis to Revelation knowledge I was receiving. My pastor was a delightful man but in spirit, a fire-breathing dragon for the Lord. The entire congregation was warm and inviting. You could not sit under this ministry and not be filled with faith or taken over, by the Holy Ghost. This is where I began to stretch spiritually. However, the adversary sees our light as it illuminates in us, as it grows and they will do whatever it takes to stop it.

My husband began to feel uncomfortable in this ministry. I found out later that he was being convicted in his spirit, just like I was, as we were beginning the 'deacon' and 'deaconess' process. It was opening him up to the evilness of his personal desires that later on, took over our marriage. But this is only an assumption, I couldn't verify this as truth, I can only attest to my own desires. I was feeling the conviction as well but I was desperately trying to accept the pruning process. I knew that my sins were many and I wanted to be free from the guilt and shame of them once and for all. But I was not prepared for what that meant nor where it would lead me.

We were at the final stages of the deacon and deaconess process in this modest ministry but we never went through with it. Instead, I allowed my husband to convince me to go elsewhere for worship service. I followed my husband to a nondenominational church wherein he felt more 'comfortable'. This is where I learned that comfort was not what the love of God was all about. In fact, it was quite the opposite.

In the wanderings of my own journey, the times when I had strayed the farthest from God were not without purpose. Living as a slave to my own sin was not all for nothing. Just as Onesimus returned to his master Philemon, free from bondage, so I returned to the Lord. Paul writes, "For perhaps [Onesimus] departed for a while for this purpose, that you might receive him forever, no longer as a slave but more than a slave, a brother especially to me but how much more to you, both in the flesh and in the Lord." (Philemon 1: 15-16). Let us keep in mind that salvation is not free. However, it does offer so many benefits. These benefits will lead us to a great life of abundance if we are willing to take the journey and do the necessary work needed to be free from the bondage of our fleshly sins.

Introduction

In this book, we are going to do some much-needed reflection on the promises of God and the chains that still hold many of us captive. I will also provide clear and precise detail of how the word of God still leads and directs us through free will. If one was only able to receive the promises of God, they would be whole. This will be a journey you never knew you needed but will elate you for having taken it. If, "You never know where you're going if you don't know where you've been" was a book, this would be it.

No matter a person's race, each person must break apart the chains of slavery in his or her life. These chains may not be visible to the naked eye. However, each person has the ability to break free from slavery or remain under a slave mentality. The key to breaking free is understanding the Word of God and having him align your thoughts and desires with his. Through the Word of God, we learn that the promises for our lives have yet to be fulfilled and abundance awaits us all if we are only able and willing to listen and hear. Post that, committing to doing the *work* it takes to access our collective heritage.

We have rejected what God has provided through his word because of the source in which it was given. The Bible has been used as a tool to distort a promise and destroy mindsets, which has impacted history in a prodigious way. The Word of God was inspired by God to give direction, embolden hope and reveal a higher plan for mankind. However, man has taken what was once pure and used it to manipulate a system that made slaves out of some and oppressors out of others.

We are still missing a vital piece of the puzzle in this game of life that has come to rob us from who we really are in this world. This fact cannot be pushed away with time, covered up by fear, nor can it be erased through history. We must come toe-to-toe with the ugly truth of the matter and lay it all out on the theoretic table to correct the imperfections of what our history has created before we can move forward into the unity which

God meant for us all. Those who know and accept this clearly get it and those who refuse will undoubtably be left behind but either way, the truth must be told.

When we pay close attention to where we come from, become intuitive of ourselves, fluent in who we are as people, and accept whose we are, we will be able to fully understand and see the systems for what they are and break that cycle. You will find it all in this manuscript through the meeting of the minds.

Many people walk around claiming to be 'woke', but our eyes have not been fully open. There are many mentalities that cause us to stay in a state of confusion through fear of stepping out into the unknown. The slave mentality is one that has been imparted by master planners who studied the consciousness of mankind. With the hypothesis and theory in hand, it was carried out precisely through trial and testing of cultural differences and determination to gain control over others. The indigenous people of the USA have been affected by these systems divulged by those who were also trained in the mindset of labor-induced tendencies and superiority.

We speak life and death through our thoughts, the way we see one another and respond to situations—be it negative or positive. If we were to rehearse the promises of God to be free from this psychological framework that was forced on us, we would receive our birthright. The promises have yet to be fulfilled. There is still hope. Within each of us, there lies a power so strong, so capable of freeing us from the bondage of our minds.

We have lost focus on the things that truly matter in this world. We have flawlessly allowed our children to fall prey to vicious cycles of slavery. We have opened the floodgates to our eyes, ears and mouth and therein, orchestrated our own web of deceit and demise. However, there is hope for the future.

The key of free-will has been given to us through the Word of God, helping us unlock these mysteries we chase. The answers to our inquiries are there, but we often refuse to study and approve ourselves in the eyes of the God (2 Timothy 2:15). We have settled for mediocracy for far too long. It is now time to dive into something that has been there all along. It is time to open the door to true opportunity and endless possibilities by unleashing the weapon that we have each carried on the inside without license. Defined by their own measures, the power of true freedom is afforded to each individual. You have access to an entire arsenal; all you need is the key to unlock it.

Turn my heart toward your statutes and not toward selfish gain. Turn my eyes away from worthless things; preserve my life according to your word.

(Psalm 119: 36-37)

Be careful, the heart tells it all. God knows our intentions. He is well aware of what we say and do. The true meaning behind our actions is tucked away from everyone else but God reads it all. He knows our plans and goals. He is well aware of those thoughts we don't share with others. However, as we become less self-involved and more driven the word of God transforms us. God's plan begins to manifest through us and shape our lives. His plan supersedes ours every time without fail. For these reasons be careful of the things you pray for and the reasons behind the prayer. And consider tangible items won't satisfy us however the word promises to sustain us forever.

Dear LORD my God,
    Let those that wish to hear, hear your voice. Allow those that wish to do, do your will. Teach those that wish to speak, speak your promises. Guide those that wish to go, to go with you. Give peace to those who seek chaos. Offer love to those who are lost in hatred. These

things I pray in your precious son Jesus' (Yahshua) name.

   AMEN

(These pages are inserts from C. Sims personal Journal)

CHAPTER 1

Wake up America

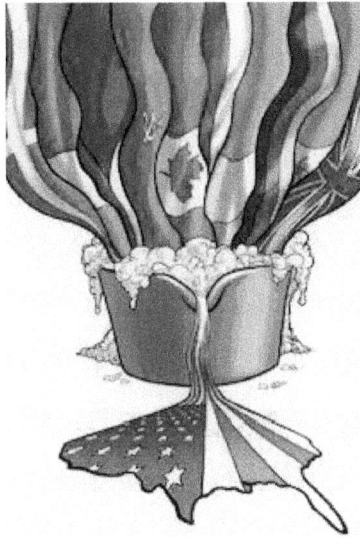

O ur conversations would always start with what seemed to be genuine concern for my well-being, inevitably ending up unbalanced and unsettling to my spirit. My mother-in-law would often tell me about how older men would love to have a beautiful young woman in their arms, that they would take care of me and give me material things. She would often talk to me about how I could go about being a mistress to some older wealthy man. I couldn't really understand the source of her conversations. Many times, I would avoid being alone with her to have these particular encounters but when the opportunity presented itself, here we were. The ride to the west side seemed to take longer than usual. She was driving while grooming me to live a life of sin. I now believe that she may have been trying to prepare me for what she would consider my destiny after my marriage with her son. All too often, these conversations would be exhausting to dwell upon or even to repeat to anyone. I chose to ignore these early signs of discord, never really realizing how it would play such a vital part in my life later on.

Our mind is often enticed by the pleasures we seek. These pleasures include happiness, entertainment, enjoyment, ecstasy, and euphoria. Once we receive one or more of these pleasures, they seem to lose their luster, leaving us disappointed. Unlike how being in nature, eating healthy, exercising, and positive thinking pleases us. The pleasures we seek are within. We must however, evaluate our thoughts. What are you thinking of? What are your thoughts on the things outside of you? Are you responding from a trained mindset or a slave mentality? Our thoughts give us the consent to pursue or retreat from situations we come in contact with. We cannot find happiness in mere possessions or materialistic things. We do not realize that it's been lying within us this whole time. The innermost thoughts matter far more than what's outside of us.

This has somehow been lost in transition of who we really are as people. We have been under foot for so long that we have lost our true identity. We have been convinced that the one thing we need in our lives is no longer a factor. We have been fed a lie that keeps on feeding itself. The lie keeps multiplying and recreating itself. There's a saying that comes to mind, "Many fish have been fillet believing a lie". When we look at history, there are key factors that we never take into consideration. In the black man's search for freedom and equality, we find a few missing tools that are needed to be completely free from the mindset of a slave. The renewing of our mind is one, forgiveness is another, while prayer and thanksgiving are yet others.

I watched a video on social media once where the host stated that, "The slaves were not *ready* to be free". That one word 'READY' took on a meaning for some. This statement alone proved his very point as the comment section blew up in fury. Those who watched the video were outraged at that statement alone. As I understood his point completely, I thought that maybe a change in that one word would have gotten a better response from his followers. If, in fact he had stated that slaves were not *prepared* to be freed, he would have been called a genius and the comments would have agreed with his statement. In the video, the host spoke on how the mental state of being free was not available to those born into slavery. They were not aware of the state of mind freedom gives. They had no idea that their freedom from one oppressor would only introduce them to another. Had they known that the industrial industry was focusing on the field hands to evolve them from one labor to another, things could have been different.

If they were aware that their freedom would offer hatred instead of equality, bring envy and jealousy to their doorstep—many would have taken the provision to protect themselves and their families. Even those who believed they operated as free men in different arenas of their lives by building cities that functioned like well-oiled machines.

Black Wallstreet was the wealthiest African American community during its time. Located in the Greenwood District in Tulsa, Oklahoma, it experienced the Tulsa massacre in 1921, where a mob of white residents, armed by city officials, attacked black residents and businesses destroying an entire community and confiscating their land and property. It's recognized as one of the worst tragedies of racial violence in American history. Black Wallstreet was the prime example of what mentally evolved men could accomplish when left to their own devices. However, even this lacked the force to sustain itself in areas regarding racial tensions.

While African Americans in the Reconstruction Era proved to many that they could obtain favor in areas of social economics, they did not think to form a system of defense against those who would find this threatening. Even post setting the bar in other arenas of life, this country sought to tear down their efforts through other means. Being prepared in the battle of our minds has been the challenge. The generational curse that was spoken of, throughout our lives was the one thing we did not take into consideration once the Emancipation Proclamation was introduced.

All along, the forefathers of this country had a plan that outlasted slavery. The area of the plan that we came in on, while kicking and screaming, was always part of the initial plan. It was to always to keep us under foot as the borrowers, or the tail. However, I am here to tell you that now is the time for this line to turn around. In my experience as a teacher, I would often have my students line up by assigning them a line leader. There were times when students thought that as a line leader, they had to be better than the other students and should be deemed worthy of the title. When that happened, I would ask everyone in the line to turn around. This request gave that student at the end of the line the opportunity to be the leader, instead of the humble caboose. The first shall become last and the last shall become first. There is no way around, it is the

Word of God. It stands on its own with no need for support.

There is an undeniable fact that God has given man dominion over their lives. In free will, we are governed by the laws of the universe while doing what we want to. There is so much power in our thoughts, words and what our heart desires. We have missed the mark in that regard. God intended for us to rule the earth over the air, seas and land. However, we refuse to acknowledge our own gift of procession. We often think thoughts of destruction, and watch our lives take form through the root of our thoughts and words.

This is comparable to a pregnant mother telling herself she will have a healthy baby, and then preparing for the opposite of what she speaks. She manifests that of what she feels deep down. Our subconscious does not distinguish from what we believe and hope. Any fear, any doubt, any form of concern comes naturally if we operate through things other than faith.

We still see ourselves as mere men, when in fact we have everything we need to succeed, within us. All we must do is reexamine how we think and what we place in our hearts. The thoughts deep down are what will flow through our lips. It's that simple. The only time it is not that simple is if you are unwilling to dismiss everything you have ever learned or told yourself.

As people, we have dismissed the idea of God and his son (Yahshua) Jesus, because of how we were introduced to God. I would like you to give me the opportunity to tell you the same story in a way that has never been told before. If you would allow me a few moments of your life to elaborate on a topic that has been tossed from one end of the spectrum to another, I may be able to open your mind. I will show you through biblical text, US history, personal circumstances and natural events; how we have been in a powerful position and were so blissfully unaware.

There are many books printed on this very matter, but none have been told like this. The discovery from this day forward will change your entire life, but only if its message is received. Let not your troubled heart fail you, for the thoughts upon it is what will heal you completely.

The spirit of God lives in each of us. We do not need further proof than our own words. Our words and thoughts produce actions which yield results. We have to see the purpose within ourselves. Waking up each day, we have an opportunity for new mercies. These mercies are granted to us and for us. Forgive yourselves and others and keep the forgiveness moving. We often times mistake what we read for what we heard. The word of God was given to allow us the opportunity to gain what was lost.

Church isn't doing it for us. Organized religion has missed the mark. The spiritually inclined must speak up. If you have found this gift, don't hide it under a bush (Matthew 5:15). Instead allow everyone around to acknowledge the concept as well. This is not meant to be hidden away, it's meant to be multiplied and shared with those who will listen. God is an intentional God. He has provided a way of escape for all who wish to be freed through his son Jesus Christ (1 Corinthians 10:13).

I believe that slavery was meant to save a nation of people who were being destroyed. Once, while having a conversation with my brother, I expressed this as a deep belief. I generally keep religion and politics at bay during family gatherings, however, that night, the topic of slavery was on the table. So, I voiced my concern for the subject matter unlike others in the conversation. My ideas at the time seemed unbelievably insane. However, I stood on my word. I believed that slavery was the result of greed for most. It was also the result of salvation for a nation that was internally dying because of their thought process and pride. You can't be too arrogant nor too naive to understand this at all. You must be balanced to see where this logic comes from. Men originated in Africa. Black men have been hated throughout history. Black men were threatening to those who did not understand them. But the black man was creating a world of evil in the land of Africa, so much so that they turned on themselves and sold one another into bondage. For those who had survived the journey, it was both a blessing and a curse. Black men have lived through centuries of abuse, yet strive for excellence. What if it's possible, that they were captured physically just to be freed mentally?

As people, we have taken the word of God and studied it in theological terms, but we have not yet grasped the true meaning of this word. We have not totally given into its infinite possibilities and opportunities. We prefer to pick and choose which part of the Bible to glean from, and which to ignore. Some have even been able to comprehend the secrets through the pages of the bible and refuse to share what they have found. When we begin to take off the blinders, share what we have found, and implement what we've learned, only then will we start to see a new world.

For the time will come when people will not put up with sound doctrine. Instead, to suit their own desires, they will gather around them a great number of teachers to say what their itching ears want to hear. They will turn their ears away from the truth and truth aside to myths. But you, keep your head in all situations, endure hardship, do the work of the evangelist, fulfilling all the duties of your ministry.

Harvesting faith is something many don't care to acquire in life. It comes with too much risk or responsibility and not enough assurance of a positive outcome. But it prevails if developed with good intentions. We do actually reap what we sow. Our faith is what keeps us going through times of hardship. There wouldn't be healing without it nor would there be any hope for the future. God has a plan for our lives. His plans are for each of us to prosper, not to harm but to give hope to a brighter future.

Dear LORD

Let me not be carried away by this myth of false doctrine instead, show me the way, teach me the truth, and shine your light within me so that I may follow you. I don't even trust my own judgements but through you I am completely depended upon. Lead me

as I carry on. In your matchless son Jesus' (Yahshua) name I pray.
AMEN.

(These pages are inserts from C. Sims personal Journal)

CHAPTER 2

Made in the USA

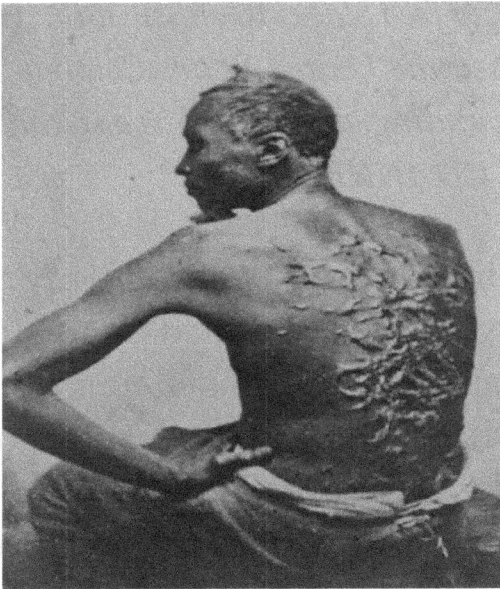

Gordon, or "Whipped Peter" (fl. 1863), was an enslaved African American who gained his freedom when he reached the Union camp near Baton Rouge. He became

known as the subject of photographs documenting the extensive scarring of his back from whippings received in slavery. Abolitionists distributed these carte de visit photographs of Gordon throughout the United States and internationally to show the abuses of slavery. In July 1863, these images appeared in an article about Gordon published in Harper's Weekly, the most widely read journal during the Civil War. The pictures of Gordon's scourged back provided Northerners with visual evidence of the brutal treatment of slaves and inspired many free blacks to enlist in the Union Army. Gordon joined the United States Colored Troops soon after their founding, and served as a soldier in the war. (HISTORY CHANNEL)

During the times spent with my mother-in-law, it hadn't dawned on me to question, that if these were her conversations with me than what would her conversations with her son look like. As parental guides, we are not fully aware of the power of life and death we hold in our tongues. Nor are we completely responsible in the use of that power and the effects it may have on our children regardless of whether they are minor or adult. Every child wants to please their mother. My husband was definitely not an exception to this rule as his mother was his bible. If her words to me cut, then I am certain those same thoughts were spoken to him under her guidance as well. Instead of communicating for clarity, assumptions were made to fester opinions and hurtful actions. You can never take back what was said but you can learn from the mistakes that result in scars which sometimes, leave us bedridden unto death.

Our history is a collage of scars from our ancestors. Thoughts of how to do something is passed down from generation to generation. The torch was handed to us to do with it what we please, based on our own perceptions. And with each new offspring comes a new way to tweak an old ideology. We currently live in a society where men have the opportunity to become whatever he puts his mind to, literally. All have a chance of entrepreneurship, career in any field, advanced education among other things. We can not only give to others and create a community of love; we can do so with the power coursing through our veins. However, to achieve this, we must let go of the anger and hurt of our past. We must allow those wounds to heal, and take the responsibility of breaking these generational curses that were put on our communities and families. We were trained to be who we are today by all the influences in our lives that we have repeated with our own thoughts and words. This is how the curse is formed which continues to spread, rapidly through our lives and the lives of our loved ones. What we speak of defines us, develops us. Your thoughts and words await manifestation. One's choice of words are vital to the meditation to their heart, mind and soul. What we tell ourselves about ourselves is who we are. And words coming off our mouths onto another define our inner selves.

Speaking the truth can sometimes hurt if the intent is to hurt. Absolutely nothing should be said if the intent is not filtered through love. The filter determines if the words speak life or death. Monitoring our own thoughts guide us while opening our door to effective communication in any situation. Gently allowing the tongue to be led by the heart partnered in agreement with the mind gives way to understanding. The past is not to be forgotten; however, we must now learn from those pre-existing things to create what is new within each of us. Doing this will usher us towards a new horizon thereby, setting forth a new era for mankind.

The adversary (1 Peter 5:8) has led us to believe that we are powerless to its forces and that we have no dominion within ourselves. We have been tricked into being complacent complainers. This entity has used all of its tricks to cause us to speak death over ourselves and those we love. It's in our music, literature, on our tv screens and surrounds our communities as well. If we concentrate on those instead of feeding our souls the truth, we are perpetuating a process that triggers the training of a slave. We no longer need slave masters to beat us into submission. We have taken this responsibility on ourselves. We the people, have been part of a systematic trend designed to enforce control beyond generations. It's time to allow what was used for bad to be used for good.

We are empowered to finally break the chains of oppression. This is the final chapter for those that wish to be free. It is the final piece of the puzzle.

There are four stages to sleep: the waking stage, light sleep, deep sleep, and REM sleep. Each stage repeats itself throughout the sleep process.

The stage between being awake and light sleep is where you are if you are obsessed with slavery not being our history. You may not want to face the fact that the declaration of a process was designed to change the way in which we think. We have learned to hate what was meant to be saved. We have rejected the word of God for so long because of the one that introduced it to us. We have taken offense to the very thing meant to save our dying souls from hurt, harm and danger. If we use this opportunity to absorb the truth, we would see the turn of a new era.

Have you ever been awake and alert but still sleep? We all have. You are awoken to be unresponsive, through several systematic instruments and industries. Have you noticed that there are numerous ways to be entertained these days? We have special televised outlets that we can enjoy from the comfort of our living room. Pick your poison. If you are an artist, you have a variety of musical genres to choose from. If you happen to prefer nonfiction over fiction, you have a plethora of reality tv shows at your service. There are game shows, news shows, cooking shows that are all available at a click of a button. There are blogs and talk shows for entertainment. We have turned away from things that give us power over every situation, to those which numb us and allows us to be desensitized to what reality truly is.

Many may feel we are all on the same playing field, and from a narrow perspective, we are. However, I challenge us all to widen our lenses to see the bigger picture—one that may hurt at first but if left unexamined, it will most certainly continue to run rapid in our communities. It will become another story like that of Whipped Peter. Until we become aware of the foul actions stemming from racism, we will not possess the ability to reach others across the country who either unknowingly or unwillingly are aware of how to change it.

I understand that at this point, you have many doubts and questions. Many of us have allowed our past to rule too much of our present. Where it was meant to make us stronger, we have willingly stayed broken. This is evident through the increase in mental health illnesses such as Depression, Bipolar disorder, Personality disorders, Dementia, Alzheimer's, and many more. Many don't believe in seeking professional assistance during the onset of these illnesses.

Therefore, they don't receive the necessary aid. Also, for good reason, African Americans have a stigma towards seeking assistance, largely due to how they were traumatically broken mentally to become slaves, evident through research and studies.

In any forum, the subject of slavery is often shrugged off as a thing of the past. People rarely care to discuss it, let alone analyze it. I often find myself asking others willing to discuss this subject matter; if they have ever read the 'Willie Lynch letter'. More often than not, they tell me that they haven't. No matter how many times I hear their answer, I am always bewildered at how anyone can bypass such an intricate and detailed documentation of how an entire race of people were programed. How do we reprogram, break the cycle, or debug a system when we are not aware of how it was created? To rid ourselves of a noisy pestilence we must first start at the root of it. I invite you to read and examine the letter at the center of slavery:

Willie Lynch Letter

Gentlemen

I greet you here on the bank of the James River in the year of our lord, one thousand seven hundred and twelve. First, I shall thank you, the gentlemen of the of the colony of Virginia, for bringing me here. I am here to help you solve some of your problems with slaves. Your invitation reached me in my modest plantation in the West Indies where I have experimented with some of the newest and still the oldest method for control of slaves. Ancient Rome would envy us if my program is implemented. As our boat sailed south on the James River, named for our illustrious KING JAMES, whose BIBLE WE CHERISH, I saw enough to know that our problem is not unique. While Rome used cords or wood as crosses for standing human bodies along the old highways in great numbers, you are here using the tree and the rope on occasion.

I caught the whiff of a dead slave hanging from a tree a couple of miles back. You are losing valuable stock by hangings, you are having uprisings, slaves are running away, your crops are sometimes left in the fields too long for maximum profit, you suffer occasional fires, your animals are killed, Gentleman,...You know what your problems are; I do not need to elaborate. I am not here to enumerate your problems, I am here to introduce you to a method of solving them.

In my bag, I have a fool proof method for controlling your slaves. I guarantee everyone of you that if installed it will control the slaves for at least three undred years. My method is simple, any member of your family or any OVERSEER can use it.

I have outlined a number of differences among the slaves, and I take these differences and make them bigger. I use FEAR, DISTRUST, and ENVY for control purposes. These methods have worked on my modest plantation in the West Indies, and it will work throughout the SOUTH. Take this simple little list of differences and think about them. On the top of my list is "AGE" but it is only there because it starts with an "A"; The second is "COLOR" or shade; there is INTELLIGENCE, SIZE, SEX, SIZE OF PLANTATION, ATTITUDE of owner, whether the slaves live in the valley, on a hill, east or west, north, south, have fine or coarse hair, or is tall or short. Now that you have a list of differences, I shall give you an outline of action- but before that, I shall assure you that DISTRUST IS STRONGER THAN TRUST, AND ENVY IS STRONGER THAN ADULATION, RESPECT OR ADMIRATION.

The black slave, after receiving this indoctrination, shall carry on and will become self-refueling and self-generating for hundreds of years, maybe thousands. Don't forget you must pitch the old black vs. the young black males, and the young black male against the old black male. You must use the dark skinned slaves vs. the light skin slaves. You must use the female vs the male, and the male vs, the female. You must always have your servants and OVERSEERS distrust all blacks, but it is necessary that your slaves trust and depend on us.

Gentlemen, these kits are your keys to control, use them. Never miss an opportunity. My plan is guaranteed, and the good thing about this plan is that if used intensely for one year the slave will remain perpetually distrustful.

william lynch 1775

Those who are kind benefit themselves while the cruel ruin themselves. The wicked deceit while the righteous sow rewards. The righteous attain life while those pursuing evil find death. The Lord detests those whose hearts are perverse but delights in those who are blameless. The wicked shan't be unpunished whereas the righteous will go free. (Proverbs 11:17-21).

The injustices of slavery carry many consequences which, if not addressed, will continue to plague those that had a hand in the narrative (Revelation 22:18-19). Through the fear of rebellion, slave owners worried that sharing the Holy Bible with slaves would encourage the pursuing of freedom and equality. Therefore, the slave bible was created. Allowing slaves to have a copy of select portions of the bible that highlighted submission and servitude further drove the agenda of superiority among slave owners. Ninety percent of the old testament and fifty percent of the New Testament was completely removed to create the slave bible. Many scriptures such as "See to it that no one takes you captive by philosophy and empty deceit, according to human tradition, according to the elemental spirits of the world, and not according to Christ" from Colossians 2:8 (ESV), would not have promoted obedience among slaves therefore it (among many others), was omitted off the slave bible. Just as the slaves were transformed mentality, physically, and spiritually, so were the slave masters. Their faint of generational curses is even more severe (James 3:1). There is nothing hidden that will remain concealed, everything will be brought out to the open. Consider carefully how you will listen for those who will, will be given more. (Luke 8:17-18).

However, once taught, we too are held accountable for our actions (1 Timothy 6:5). What we do now means everything. We should foster hope; for no matter what has happened in our past, we are now free to choose a direction. Many have rejected the word of God and turned their backs on following doctrines of any kind. Whether you are a Christian or not, the signs and wonders of the world today cannot be denied nor shooed away by small-minded concepts. The enemy despises things that cause us to dig deeper to better understand the particulars and concepts of the Word of God. He would rather we remain ignorant and naive to his devices long enough to cause all of us to miss our mark. This is not the end. Remember, God always provides a ram in the bush for those he loves.

I pray that none of us miss the call. That through the parables of Jesus Christ, we all acknowledge and understand that it's time to see the clarity in what was meant to be hidden from us.

He restores my soul; he leads me on the path of righteousness for his name's sake.

(Psalm 23: 3)

Restoration is known as an action of returning something to its former owner, place, or condition. The development of wholeness has a way of stripping us down completely and reconstructing who we are. The things we would have done—we no longer do and vice versa. In self-restoration, we gain knowledge of what the outcome has been, while we are renewed. God has a way of fixing us for his glory. He knows the areas we fall short in, but he also knows that those very same shortcomings can be used for our own good. Being self-absorbed in our faults only bring worry, stress, and fear. I come to encourage you to fear not brothers and sisters, for God knows exactly what he is doing. We must just allow the process to complete itself.

Dear Lord,
Thank you for being the lifter of my head. I am your child dear God and I know you love me. I vow to go where you will have me go. I will do what you will have me do. I will say what you will have me say. I will not fear nor listen to the noisy pestilence. I will remember that no matter where I am, you would take

care of the birds in the air, that you will also care for
me. In Jesus' (Yahshua) most holy name.
   AMEN.

(These pages are inserts from C. Sims
personal Journal)

CHAPTER 3

Consider the Source

Many times, as parents, we fail to see how our response to our children's wrongdoings cause them to find other ways to do the very thing you are trying to teach them not to do. We all know how to adapt well in areas that are meant to please us. Neo-Confederates share idealistic goals to preserve what is known as the southern culture, which stemmed from the slave era. This group stands against the removal of Confederate monuments and honor the confederate flag with many members sharing views and ties with white supremacy groups as well. This particular flag has been the sentiment flag for the state of Mississippi for decades. Today, the state is sketching a new design intended for the flag. Changes also include removal of the Confederate statues. These plans are intended to pacify a culture and to erase fault of this country as they uphold the deniability clause of its ancestral guilt. The memorials represent a time wherein intimidation and manipulation over a group was needed to "keep them in line". However, no one is willing to address the real offence or come to the table with the complete truth of the matter. How did a nation get built on the back of slaves with no place in history that accounts for this? How is it that thousands were wiped out, left forgotten in what now rests as an orchard of peaches? No removal of effigies will account for what was lost. However, if one were to question why it's imperative that these be disregarded, they would find that digging deeper leads to ugly hidden stains left undiscovered. Like that of the Devils Punch Bowl in Natchez, Mississippi, where free slaves were forced into concentration camps by the Union Army and left to die once they were deployed during the civil war. What accounts do we have for the 20,000 lives lost there?

It is my belief that someone took a look at the historical facts and realized a grave error made during slavery that needed rectification. African American people were brought to this country to be endowed servants to people who considered themselves as superior. These spoiled brats implemented methods that were flawed and corrupt. The slave masters often found it within themselves to quote the Bible to justify their actions. They used the very thing meant to save; to enslave. They took the word inspired by God and the promises given, and twisted it to their advantage. Through the study of the

Bible, it was known to all who 'the lost tribe of Zion' were. However, in efforts to discard this information, words were removed, replaced, and redirected. With this being done, we find that many have rejected the word of God because of the incomplete truth displayed throughout the pages. While carefully studying the word of God, we discover the ultimate truth. Analyzing this precisely makes us aware of what we need to know.

I believe that there were people compelled to spread the word of God to all who would listen, to enlighten the slaves through the Holy Bible. The cultural knowledge was stripped from the hearts and minds of those taken from their homeland wherein lies the origin of the book. Yet, here we are. People question the possibility of how the Bible; used as a source to keep one in chains, could be used to set many free instead. The secret has been hidden between its pages for years. We are surrounded by people designed to tell us the truth, but we are also tasked with the responsibility to find the truth ourselves (2 Timothy 2:15). This is where many of us fall short.

Throughout my life, I have always been accused of over-analyzing situations and circumstances. I always found myself asking questions when presented with a problem, or even a solution to a problem. It has always been like this, but those close to me always pointed out their issues with it. A pastor once told me that the Lord could not possibly use me due to my analytical brain. He thought I analyzed too much during any conversation. Having heard this about myself before, I immediately took the inquiry to the Lord in prayer. I asked him to show me why I analyzed everything and if it was a good thing or a bad thing for me to act so. He revealed to me that this given trait could be put to use. The Holy Spirit led me to 2 Timothy 2. When I realized that the word "analyze" is in fact the synonym for the word "study", I began to understand who I was in Christ through the meaning of my government name. I am Christine Renee, Christian Reborn.

Seek and you shall find, knock and the door shall be open. It is true that whatever we ask for; if it is the will of God, it shall be done.

The Bible has become the basis for how one should live their life, yet it is the most unused form of Literature. Just like our minds, the majority of the content in the bible is untapped or misunderstood. Philosophers have analyzed and depicted the content of both the mind and the Bible. New religions have been formed to interpret its meaning, yet they adopt a few of its concepts. However, no one has come close to realizing that the tool that has been given is a formulated version of what was created by God. These books convey the highest form of intelligence made by our Lord and Savior Yahweh to direct us to the core of who we are within ourselves; to fulfill the purpose of our creation. Everything works in favor of those who love the Lord. Everything we need in order to be the men and women of God, is already within us (Romans 8:28). We must find the road map to get to the appointed destination.

"As a man think in his heart, so is he" (Proverbs 23:7) suggests that our thoughts give way to what is in our hearts. This is vital information that unlocks opportunities and possibilities. This is how God knows our hearts. He knows what lies beneath the surface of the life-changing experiences we encounter, and how they have shaped what we say, what we do and how we think.

God knows our heart; he knows what drives us and what motivates us. Proverbs (21:2) tells us, "but the Lord weighs the heart". He gives us the tools needed to build his kingdom. It is our duty to break the generational curse that hindered our ancestors. Our children and our children's children need to know the blueprint of salvation governing the world we live in. We are no longer seeking to hold one another back from the truth through personal gain, sugarcoated words and clever phrases. We have a job to do—a job that demands us to get our minds right based on our hearts' intentions. Our hearts and minds need to align together as one. "When we do good, good follows us" (Psalm 23:6). While being optimistic, positivity and good fortune chases us down. "All these blessings will come on you and accompany you if you obey the lord, your God" (Deuteronomy 28:2). The same applies to negativity. This is what reaping and sowing reveals to us. When you sow good seeds, you reap a good harvest, it's that simple. Instead, if you sow bad seeds, good luck getting anything useful. When we say things like, "the same old, same old" after someone asks us how we are doing, we are internalizing this pattern. We are making a conscious decision, a declaration if you will, to have the same thing we've always had. Let go of the same old stinking thoughts and embrace something new. We should no longer wish to just be among the land of the living. We must strive to live up to what's been promised to us, an abundant life.

Who we are in life depends solely on what we put our faith in. Many times, we are transformed from one mentality to another based on those we surround ourselves with. We conform to the belief of what others think of us, instead of developing who we are for ourselves. This, however, sets the tone for our success or failure. There are two sides to every coin, of course. We would like to choose the better version of ourselves, but the way we think can cause us to fall back to our dominant version without putting up a fight. What if we all possessed the ability to change the outcome merely by believing it's possible and that we have that capability?

We were all raised differently therefore, our perceptions and thoughts differ. Not one person is inferior than another, we are unique. Our thought process shapes us and all we do. How we react and respond to situations beyond our control, how we do simple household chores, how we interact with others etc. in our daily lives is who we are. We internalize this from childhood to adulthood, and pass them onto another generation, tweaking the things we wish to change based on our experience.

An example: As a child, I woke up early every Christmas morning to open gifts from Santa. As time passed and I grew up, I realized there was no Santa. I thought how silly it was to be so nervous the night before, unable to fall asleep and yet fearful I would be caught awake. As a child, Christmas time was not my favorite for it introduced me to my anxiety. Although the large number of gifts I opened the next day made up for the night before, I would be exhausted, having to push myself to interact with my family and loved ones. As an adult, I was pleased that my husband's family to the idea of opening a single gift from under the tree on Christmas Eve. We added a Christmas Eve dinner gathering with our loved ones so that on Christmas morning, the excitement of being with one another was the focus instead of focusing on Santa. As an adult, I created something for my children to prevent them from experiencing the feelings I did, during the holiday season as a child.

The mind is a powerful tool that often remains untapped. Many people function on autopilot during holidays due to their beliefs, culture, traditions and upbringing. They do the same things their parents did in the same way, sometimes even settling in the same old town they grew up in. They often think it's strange when they meet someone who is different from them in other areas of life and wonder how they managed to get by. It is rare to see people willing to open themselves up in anyway. They may acknowledge the chances awaiting them, but will never volunteer to venture out of their comfort zones. The most important reason though, is the fear of the unknown. Fear can be crippling. Our thoughts of who we are and how we are supposed to be is the blueprint to how we live. But what if I told you that the way you think, and have been thinking all your life, is wrong?

I understand the shock that comes along with that statement. I boldly and unapologetically will say it again so it's clear. The way you have been thinking all your life, is wrong. Now hear me out and once you do, you can decide on whether you want to continue reading.

In the black community, families for years have multiplied and increased, going from the slave masters' plantation to home and business owners to influential pillars of society. These families have truly evolved in many ways. All except one: the way of elevational thinking.

We, often times hear the word "woke", used to mean we are enlightened and know who we truly are. However, in being "woke", many of us have yet to open our eyes to the truth. And like most strong-minded people, we shut down anything that tells us otherwise, and dismiss the truth—even if it is meant to heal us.

In 1712, on the banks of the James River in Virginia, William Lynch gave a mesmerizing speech that changed the nation and corrupted the process of our thoughts. The process; spoken by Mr. Lynch himself and I quote, "I guarantee every one of you that, if installed correctly, it will control the slaves for at least 300 years."

Many refuse to look into this as they feel it no longer had any valid purpose or relevance to the process of our thinking. But I am here to prove them wrong. Not only does it have validation, it also has the key to unlocking these chains that have held us captive for generations. The only thing needed to obtain it, is an open mind.

There are people in this world who feel that we should allow the past to stay in the past but these people are part of a manipulative system that was created to make us forget the experiences endured by generations on end. We must not ignore it but allow it to help us grow, using it as a catalyst to embrace unity in diversity. When you open up a thing to dissect why it performs the way it does, you find crucial details in the hidden parts.

Our thoughts have been altered making us differ from who we were intended to be, from the creation of time. We wonder why so many people are poor and angry. Or why there is so much violence in our cities. Well, there is a formula that has been followed for over 300 years that we ourselves have been cultivating in our families and culture through generation to generation. It is time to break the curse. It is no longer acceptable for some to be freed and not all. Reach one, teach one and forsake no one is the ultimate goal.

The breaking training lessons were taught to ensure slaves remain loyal. Being freed from slavery was only to put to test the ideals indoctrinated during slavery. The release of slaves only opened up a generation that enslaves itself and does not evolve mentally. There is evidence of this lingering in many areas of this country. So much was lost as we have fallen to the waste side. We often wonder why the African Americans are still fighting for rights that are given freely to others. Well, think about it. The slave was trained to be free to work accordingly for his master without force.

And at midnight. Paul and Silas prayed, and sang praises unto God: and the prisoners heard them. And suddenly, there was a great earthquake, so that the foundations of the prison were shaken: and immediately all the doors were opened, and every one's chains came loose. And the keeper of the prison awakening out of his sleep, and seeing the prison doors open, he drew out his sword, and would have killed himself, supposing that the prisoners had fled. But Paul cried with a loud voice, saying, Do thyself no harm: for we are all here. Then he called for a light, and sprang in, and came trembling, and fell down before Paul and Silas....

(Acts 16:25-29)

Quite often, people ask themselves if they can trust God. However, we should be asking ourselves—can God trust us instead. The Lord will not put more on us than we can bear but will, with the temptation, make a way of escape, that we may be able to endure it. Because the sufferings of this world are temporary and not worthy to be compared to the glory which is to come. Paul and Silas experienced firsthand, a mighty move of God. Because God is the same now as he was then and forever more. We too, can encounter such a blessing.

Dear Lord,

Remove that which is broken and replace anything that is missing within me. If there is anything that is blocking me from doing your will, take it away. Heal me from within and complete me furthermore. In Jesus' (Yahshua) name, I pray.

Amen

(These pages are inserts from C. Sims personal Journal)

CHAPTER 4

Hardwood Floors

The scripture and faith by itself, if not accompanied by action, is dead (James 2:14-26). Acknowledging you are in bondage is the first step to freedom. You begin to sample the habitual thinking of things you must restore, address, or rectify. The spiritual being begins to tug on your heart strings.

Traveling from one place to another since 9/11 has become a series of search and siege. You cannot go to the airport these days without assurance that everything is in its rightful place. There are items you cannot take onboard an airline with you. To assure that everyone is safe, we all must now undergo the experience of Transportation Security Administration (TSA). The TSA is the system of security in all airports organized to screen passengers, luggage, etc. before flights deploy. This system was put into place after a weakness was discovered in Airport security on Sept. 11, 2001.

Most of us remember, no matter where we were in the world on that day, what it felt like; watching from the nearest television screen, the horrors it inflicted on our nation. I remember seeing the reaction of President George W. Bush during this time. He was in a classroom reading stories to a group of children when he received the news of the first tower crash. The look of disbelief on his face said everything. I dare not assume anything else as there were millions who were watching the same.

'Ecclesiastes 3' comes to mind as I think about those past events. There are times in our lives wherein we should prepare for war in times of peace. However, the war I speak of here is the one in our minds. We must become the TSA of our thoughts. In today's society, we are facing not only a rise in racial tensions, but we are also faced with an unpredictable pandemic called Covid19. A new normal as many are confessing. Calling those things as though they were, I see the Corona virus as an opportunity for possibility. Perhaps, if we were to take the time to digress, we all can learn something from this. Attention mankind, this is no time to lose our heads. Revolt is the slave mentality. We have to be free in mind and in spirit. We have to know who we are.

The use of fear, distrust, and envy was the main source of mind control. This would explain why men are dying in the hands of the former mindsets. Hate is taught. It does not stand without judgment nor is it amplified without fear. If hate can be learned, it can also be unlearn. It's a mindset. When we unlearn hate, it can evolve into love. Love covers a multitude of sins (1 Peter 4:8). There's an example of what love does in the midst of hate. Hate breeds in the dark but love is light. Only light can overcome darkness. Love illuminates itself in the tunnel of hate.

I would recommend, to this world upset by the pandemic, that everyone take shelter in their own homes with peaceful protest in their own living rooms and manifest on things we wish to achieve. That of solidarity and peace in unity for a country that is our home built by the hands of our ancestors and gifted to us. In your home, you can shut down the economy, in your home, you can choose who comes and goes. The level of safety is up to you. Let's see what happens when you let go of the doom and gloom and focus on the outcome of victory that is in your minds. The battle is already at hand. One fist is the rod of salvation. Tribe of Judah stands tall in your thoughts. This is a necessary phenomenon that needs to take place for this world to finally break free from the chains of slavery. This is the last step to complete freedom.

Over the course of time, there has been one

devastation after another, rising the fear level. By creating a flight or fight circumstance, there are ways to control the narrative. However, if we would think for a moment and access the situation in our free mind—we can come to an advisable conclusion. No one is coming to our rescue for we must save ourselves. Ask yourself— how do we save ourselves? What if it's true that we are feared and the only way to suppress us is to strip us off our birthright and mentality through fear. And the words that were reformed as watered-down versions of the creator was used against us. However, those who will hear, let them hear. Turn up your defense. Click the switch in your mind that allows alignment with who you truly are. Think of the possibilities that lie before you, the medium to enable change. You no longer have to remain suppressed by your thoughts. You have the opportunity shift your life, change it for the better. What happens when you declare to live and not die? Declare to live in a world that sees you as an equal. When you give yourself means to live the life that you claim you deserve, the change begins. It's hard to fathom that your breakthrough depends solely on you. Accepting the truth can be troubling but once you acknowledge it, it will set you free.

I recall watching a movie called Limitless. It was about a man who was down on his luck and stumbled across a pill that enables him to access 100% of his brain abilities. The movie was based on the theory that we only use 10% of our brains. In the movie, once the character indulges in this drug, he gets on the top of his game, succeeding in everything he set out to do. There is a key that unlocks a portion of our mind, unfortunately it's not a random pill but mere hard work. Developing a thought process that is intentional gives us access to thoughts that would not be available otherwise given the low vibration of thinking many of us are currently in.

Holding bitterness in can lead to stains of hurt, guilt and pain. Like hard wood floors, our thoughts need to be purged to take on the beauty that's hidden within. In order to keep wood floors beautiful, we have to sand them down beyond the skiff marks and imperfection. Purging is the letting go of things that no longer serve you. Our pain often times, lingers too long and we end up nursing it back to its rightful place. The true sign that we need to let something go is the feeling we get when talking about incidents that make us relive any traumatic experience like it was yesterday. So many of us harbor our thoughts. Hoard our memories with people who no longer can offer an apology for their mistakes. We are willing to open the door to our pain as if it would offer some sort of relief, even for a moment. However, the ugliness of those stains and scoff marks on the floor are prominent in the light. The hope for tomorrow is visible nevertheless.

We have done such a disservice to the people of this country by blotting out the stain that our forefathers made. We discredited what the stain represents—a memorial of a time that should never be forgotten. If we ignore our past, how will we learn from it? There is pain in correction truly so, however, that pain can never heal itself if it's not laid out on the table to be dealt with. Not speaking of it as if it never happened is an insult to those who died so we may live. We are American, Indian, African, we are made in the USA.

The revealing of racial tensions in this country is heartbreaking but the way people are uniting is heartwarming. There are a number of things happening simultaneously in our world today. And it is clear that we are not all on the same page. If this tension has granted us an opportunity to reconcile and reconsider our actions, it can possibly direct us to the path of greater things. There is no reason why we, as civilized people, can't come together to make sure our children and grandchildren live better lives. Matthew (11:28-30) states, "Come to me, all you who are weary and burdened, and I will give you rest. Take my yoke upon you and learn from me, for I am gentle and humble in heart, and you will find rest for your souls. For my yoke is easy and my burden is light."

We often become busybodies in our own right, over analyzing and doubting our own ability and strength. When we become aware of the authority that we possess, it takes on a completely different meaning for us. We become free of boundaries and obstacles. The elevation of thought takes us on a journey through life like no other. However, it's not something you can put on like a coat but more like something you marinate in, until it's a part of you. Then and only then will you know without doubt what you are capable of. At this point, the universe leads, guides, and protects you as it maneuvers around your thoughts and emotions, eliminating all fears, and encompassing your entire existence. Wherever your feet tread, you have dominion. Whatever you touch is blessed. Your visions become reality.

As you believe, so you are. Take back your authority and release your gifts upon this Earth. The profit is guaranteed; a ten-fold return on your investment. That's a promise that will never turn void. You've tried everything else, why not try this?

The world sees us as crazy when we speak on the things God tells us through the Holy Spirit which resides within us. Why do you think that is? I believe that so many people have denied the fact that the trinity is real; that they do not or are unable to comprehend the minds of those who are in touch with the Lord. There are Christians who believe in God the Father, Jesus the Son, and the Holy Ghost however, they too cannot imagine any of the three speaking to them or anyone else for that matter.

In Corinthians (2: 2), Paul teaches us to be forgiving of those who offend us quickly so that we may triumph over things that try to defeat us, daily. It is Satan's job to try every device he has in his possession to convince us that we are no longer who God proclaims us to be. It is the darkness before the dawn. How do you truly know that you are a child of God if you are not tried or tested in the spirit? We must not be fooled or tricked into believing that because of our sinful actions, we cannot be children of the most high. I am often reminded that greater is He who is within me than he who is within the world. The Holy Spirit that resides within us often sits dormant, waiting on us to feed it. Acknowledgement of the word feeds the Holy Spirit and causes it to resound within us. The purposeful acceptance of the message of Jesus Christ allows an awakening of 1/3 of the Trinity. The Trinity consists of a three-part blessing which is that of God, Jesus, and the Holy Spirit. God sits on the throne, Jesus at his right-hand petitioning for the sinners, while the Holy Spirit is here with us. The Holy Spirit rests, resides, and rules within us only through our free will. When we allow our free will to be united with the will of God, that is when we begin to see miracles take place.

One morning, I was having a conversation with God as I sat in the Johnson's Control Plymouth plant before our morning team meeting. I worked on an assembly line with a team of all men. I often arrived early to get a good seat and to read my bible. I asked God if he could possibly provide me with a cup of orange juice this morning. My exact words were, "Lord, I just want some orange juice this morning for some reason." I do not know why I requested orange juice for apple juice had always been my first choice. But as I sat there, waiting as my coworkers begin to enter the break room, my team member Ed came in with a brown bag of bagels, a gallon of orange juice and some red cups for our team. He asked if I wanted some, I was unable to conceal the joy on my face and said, "Yes I do. Thank you, Jesus".

I found that acknowledging Jesus in every aspect of my life has caused me to walk in peace and gratitude. One way I do this is, every time I see a bird fly in my view, I say, "Thank you, Lord". It reminds me of the promise in Matthew (6:26)—"Behold the fowls of the air: for they sow not, neither do they reap, nor gather into barns; yet your heavenly Father feed them. Are ye not much better than they?". These small reminders cause me to be extremely appreciative of the life I have. I found myself thanking God for the rain when I feel the need to be washed clean, the sunshine when I am on a road trip, even down to the first three parking spaces at Target on my Sunday errand run. I try to see God in every area of my mundane life which makes it quite interesting to say the least.

This is my commandment, that you love one another, as I have loved you. Greater love has no man than this: to lay down his life for his friends.

(John 15:12-13)

"To love one another as I have loved you" said Jesus. Love is unconditional with GOD. He loves us even with all our flaws. God has seen us at our worst and accepted us as we are. No one is exempt. His love is for everyone. God shows the perfect example of a father. He also expects us to love one another unconditionally. By using the model given to love those around us, we allow Godly love to spread throughout our families and friends. This is how we bear good fruit by spreading the love of Jesus.

Dear LORD,

Create in me a clean heart and renew a right spirit in me. Give me those desires of my heart only if they line up with your will for my life. Allow your supernatural favor to fall fresh on me this day. I pray in your loving son, Jesus' (Yahshua) name.

AMEN

(These pages are inserts from C. Sims personal Journal)

CHAPTER 5

Membership vs VIP Pass

So the last shall be first, and the first last; for many are called, but few chosen.— Matthew (20:16). Having a VIP guest pass is far different from membership itself. Membership offers amenities that a guest rarely has an opportunity to enjoy. As a guest, you receive a tour of the facilities, hourly visits to use a few of the pleasures of said facility, and maybe a snack during the orientation process. The guest pass allows you to view what could possibly be yours and to hear the dialogue of the members who seem to enjoy their privileges. On the outside looking in, it seems that if you invest in this organization you too, can partake in such lovely activities and delights. So, you check the reviews for any signs of foul play, most times rationalizing any negative reviews as a one-time case scenario. You contemplate your wishful desires to be a part of the majority. You weigh the pros and cons, justifying things that seem out of focus. You calculate the cost and tally up your bill. As you sit in the guest seat of the VIP, you tell yourself with confidence that this is where you belong. Everyone upon first introductions are friendly and approachable. You enjoy your day deciding to continue with your research for the duration of your stay using your VIP guest pass for the week to its full advantage. During this time, as you come and go, you feel like a member. However, when the expiration date comes into view, you realize how the euphoria has worn off. Yet the pressure has begun to build. Membership is the key to unlock all uncertainties while providing knowledge to unanswered questions and concerns. The guest pass is revoked at the door. So, what happens next?

However, the inclusion of membership has an entirely different perspective. As a member, you not only have a seat at the table but you also have a voice for action within this society. Your membership allots you benefits that open doors to various rewards and collaborative relationships. Membership gives you networking abilities. It places you in the room with the presuming elite. Ones who, in their minds, are superior to others because of their status in affiliation with one another. Membership can offer an exclusive or paramount dignity.

While there are many ways to become a member, there is a lengthy process that is recognized once the fee is paid. Even though one's status can quickly change from a VIP or visitor to a member through funds obtained, there is a trial period that is never communicated. Nevertheless, it is laid out in the fine print of the contract and this process is lengthy and frivolous.

During the trial period, the said members begin to differ their experiences based on being a recipient with a VIP pass to a now, inclusive member of an association that welcomes them with open arms while putting them on the back burner to earn their keep while at the table.

Your voice is submerged in conversation because no one recognizes you. You don't look like the others nor do you act like the veterans they've all become accustomed to. You are in that awkward stage of being misunderstood. The ads don't seem to fit what you're now receiving as an affiliate. This isn't what you thought you were investing in. But you've written the check and you resolve to make the most of the situation you've locked yourself into. Let's take advantage of the amenities and roll on.

Just like the scenario mentioned between membership and VIP guest, the United States within its constitution has revoked the membership of a select group of people. African American citizens have strived to become members of a country that was built by their own sweat, blood, and tears. Despite the words of the supreme law of the United States, the Constitution was derived from superior view of those who did not consider all of its members or future members purposefully. The contract of empowerment and source of governing those in leadership, the constitution states: "We the People of the United States, in Order to form a more perfect Union, establish Justice, insure domestic Tranquility, provide for the common defense, promote the general Welfare, and secure the Blessings of Liberty to ourselves and our Posterity, do ordain and establish this Constitution for the United States of America." This document is supposed to lay out the fundamental rights of ALL citizens in the United States. But black people have not experienced the amenities clearly laid out in the body of the constitution. The perfect union failed them when the slave ships landed on the shore of America. The established justice has been overlooked as men, women, and children are killed in the streets of this country by the hands of others. Domestic tranquility has been null and void as mothers wail in sorrow for their sons. There is no common ground let alone common defense. General welfare is a joke based on the safety of others. The court system offers harsher punishments to African Americans to maintain the rise of the prison system which houses many black men who are free labor to the state. The Merriam Webster dictionary defines liberty as the "state of being FREE within society from oppressive restrictions imposed by authority on one's way of life, behavior, or political views". The future generation is still suffering from the ill-mannered treatment of those who have paid the price and done their unjust time for this country.

There are many times when having any membership can be the loneliest time in your life. Having to prove your loyalties to strangers by neglecting those who've been there for you through the same fight for equality; while becoming an equal member of the country you were born in, is exhausting. Our family, friends, and loved ones cheer us on as we attempt to cross into a country club set society in which we have been made to feel inequitable and discriminated against, in many forms. Many have become accustomed to this injustice and are now desensitized to it all together. Those that it does not directly affect, rationalize the mistreatment based on biases at their end of the spectrum. They chose to show favoritism instead of sound mind doctrine, vision or opinion of their own.

This country has convinced itself and others that all is well while manipulating minds and shunning those that 'don't belong'. By controlling the narrative of the development of all other groups unlike itself. Forming an amazing concept of exclusion. The VIP guest pass of slavery couldn't have possibly uncovered that. However, at that stage, the euphoria known as the Reconstruction era brought many things to light. The government reluctantly failed at protecting its newly freed citizens as stated in its constitution. When people deem you to be apart but different from the others, they introduce a bullying mentality into the scope of things, leaving innocent bloodshed in thriving communities because of jealousy and envy.

In order to understand bullying, you must first understand manipulation. We all have had experiences where we have been manipulated or are the ones manipulating. Which spectrum you've witnessed it on is not important however, what is vital are the signs. There were telltale signs that warn you when things are going against everything you believe in. Therefore, you are forced to either give in or fight against it. Many either ignore the signs or are gullible to them. When a newbie arrives on scene, it's cool for some to assert their authority while pushing buttons that may be insensitive to the new member. This mentality is one of superiority complex. One who deems themselves greater over another. This is what kept African Americans at odds with one another for centuries. 'How to make a slave' shows how dark-skinned slaves were kept for field work while the lighter skinned slaves worked in the house. All had the membership of a slave but the mentality of one being favored over another causes superiority complex disorder. This is the catalyst of what drives prejudices and instigates bullying. The most elite clubs like that of the United States have these secret societies that are at best, forces of great power wherein it's often troublesome to stand up against them.

Throughout history, there have been many people who were debarred in their own communities. The pharisees talked about Jesus spreading vicious rumors and accused him of blasphemy. In the schemes of the pharisees, God gave birth to his plan that was greater than any of them could possibly imagine.

In our walk with the Lord, we may easily find ourselves on the wrong side of a circumstance, unaware of our role in that situation. When we are the catalyst of rumors or backbiting, it's hard for us to see ourselves as such therefore, instead of considering we are wrong, we look for signs to justify our actions. This has become the infectious disease in many churches today. History repeating itself if you will. We preach about love and loving one another past our flaws but we consistently break down each other for selfish and vindictive reasons that somehow, boosts our own self-worth. I believe that if it's truly love above all as Jesus taught us, we would voluntarily choose him above our own selfishness. Unfortunately, that isn't the case. When we think about love, we forget to think that it could be as simple as love thy neighbor as thyself.

It saddens me that as children of God, we can't learn from our brother Jesus by accepting brotherly love. I can honestly say I've been guilty of this as well. We miss the good in people who are genuinely a blessing because of our own blindness to the hate we carry within us. 1 John (3:13 -17) says, "Do not marvel, my brethren, if the world hates you. We know that we have passed from death to life, because we love the brethren. He who does not love his brother abides in death.

Whoever hates his brother is a murderer, and you know that no murderer has eternal life abiding in him. Through him, we know love, because he laid down his life for us. And we also ought to lay down our lives for the brethren. But whoever has this world's goods and see his brother in need and shuts up his heart from him, how does the love of God abide in him?"

Today I am learning that above all, love is what's needed to move forward. Without it, there is no way to honestly administer to the broken and the lost. This must start in our hearts then seep into our spirit as we learn to love ourselves. Without self-love, we will be unable to love one another. Let's turn ourselves inside out to carry out God's plan for our lives. Like my First Lady says, "I love you and there's nothing you can do about it."

Those who consider themselves religious and yet do not keep a tight rein on their tongues deceive themselves, and their religion is worthless. Religion that God our Father accepts as pure and faultless is this: to look after orphans and widows in their distress and to keep oneself from being polluted by the world.

(James 1: 26-27)

Guard your words because out of your mouth speaks the depths of your heart. It is possible to observe and know what you need to know about others but until you've actually engaged in conversation, you cannot comprehend totally. God is the only one who knows our hearts but the spirit identifies the spirit in us all. A love for people is necessary as is a ministry within itself. Remember to love others as you love yourselves and be humble unto God. When speaking to others, always practice speaking positively no matter the situation.

Dear God,
   I thank you, that am not a pleaser of man but am led by you. Thank you for I am strong with you and cannot be defeated. LORD God, thank you for the covering of protection that follows me daily. I plead the blood of Jesus over my body, mind and soul. Whatever plot that has been thought of by Satan, with regards to

me has already failed and cast into the pits of hell from which it came. Because of your faithfulness, you have delivered me out of the hands of my enemies and for that, in the precious name of Jesus (Yahshua), I give you all the praise and glory.

Amen.

(These pages are inserts from C. Sims personal Journal)

CHAPTER 6

In Relationship

Church is the jump start to your faith. Religion never determines your belief in God. However, relationship with Jesus does. How much of Christ are we willing to get to know or is it simple enough to dismiss Jesus through the course of our sins? When we refuse things handed to us, introduced by a weaker but dominated source, we continue to walk in captivity. The word of God has freed us from condemnation and given us the opportunity to see ourselves for who we truly are in Christ. We just need to take the time to build a right relationship with God by confessing our sins through true repentance.

When we tell ourselves that we no longer wish to be held captive by our past nor do we wish to be oppressed through our sins, we find ourselves entering on the road to recovery. To gain freedom, we have to invite Jesus into our hearts, spend time getting closer to him through the word of God, and truly open ourselves up to change. We must stop, cease all the things we once took pleasure in.

Suddenly, the Lord will move on behalf of those who diligently seek him. In any relationship, we have to search for ways to better understand one another. Walking in each other's so to speak, by having compassion for one another. Loving, in spite of the wrongdoing. We wrestle, not against flesh and blood but against principles, against powers, against rulers of darkness of the age, against spiritual hosts of wickedness in heavenly places. Therefore, we must walk in love with one another.

I used to think relationship with men were fulfilling. I set myself up for a sin I couldn't get myself out of. I fell in love too easily and mostly just to feel something that was not love at all. I now know that the self-hate I carried stemmed from a number of things beyond my control. The road to my purpose led me through some rough terrains. But the love of God was waiting for me. Once I came to my revelation, everything about me changed. You too can be freed from a life of bondage if you only take time to reconcile yourself with Christ, knowing that only he can provide everything you are seeking. Straying away from him will only leave you feeling broken, abandon, abused, and misused.

I asked the Lord to show me my heart so I could see what he saw in me. When it was revealed, I was aware of why my intentions always seemed to fall short. I was unaware of the good that was there because I was too blinded by the things I knew about myself. I had created a prison for myself in the things I knew I've done wrong. So, then I asked him to help me clean my heart and to renew the right spirit in me. God in turn, opened me up and cleaned out every last bit of everything I was too ashamed to share. He gave me a new beginning. After all the running and hiding I had done in my life, when I finally invited God into my heart, he removed the weight I had carried making me light again. I am now able to tell my truth unapologetically and I see things with a clearer lens. This is how I found my freedom. I am certain beyond any shadow of doubt that if the Lord our God did this for me, he most certainly can do this for you as well. Acts (10:34) tells us that God does not favor individuals, which means if he would do for one, he will also do for another. God doesn't show favoritism and definitely doesn't practice nepotism for he loves us all the same.

The question is—How do you operate? In I Corinthians (8-13), the Apostle Paul speaks here what's within each of us. It is our duty as sons and daughters of God to check on ourselves and one another. Therefore, in risking repetitiveness of redundancy, I pose the question again my sisters and brothers—How do you operate?

We either operate in faith, hope, and love or we operate in doubt, fear and disdain. To operate means to follow a course of conduct that is often irregular.

Just as it's man's nature to follow routines he's always known based on his heritage, how he was raised, or who he has become individually, it is our nature as sinners to continue the things that would act as a foothold for the enemy. It is the duty of the advisory to kill, steal, and destroy. He comes after all our relationships, through our loved ones, our marriages, our friendships. Because he knows the power that lies within a bond. He understands what was meant in Amos (3:3), "How can two walk together unless they agree." He acknowledges this as a statement rather than a question. He is aware of God's promise, Matthew (18:20), "For where two or three are gathered in my name, there am I among them." The enemy's job is to break that.

Within our relationships, for example, of a husband and wife, each party must agree on how they will operate (dwell) with one another.

Their trust for one another leads them into this agreement. Many marriages fail because the agreeable bond either holds no validity or is broken in some way or another.

Such is the same in all relationships whether it be friendships, kinships, partnerships, etc. When the bond of trust is solidified, there lies an unspoken rule of care for one another.

The problem sets off when we are entertaining demons, unaware of it. When one operates from a place of jealousy or envy, the bond of brotherhood is breached and broken without warning.

The clever thing about the adversary is that once it's given a foothold of doubt, fear, or disdain, it subtly invades each area of our lives if not put in check.

While operating in the spirit of faith, hope and love, we must check ourselves daily in our thoughts, in our words, in the way we handle one another. Ask ourselves the question—what are we operating in? The word of Jesus comes to mind, "He who has ears, let him hear."

For no man that does anything in secret, and he himself seeks to be known openly. If you do these things, show yourself to the world.

(John 7:4)

God knows all. It is indeed a promise that he sits high and looks low. We would think that fact alone would be enough to detour us from doing wrong. But it does not. If there is anything hidden it will come to the light. Many times, we take on biases from others that lead us to a process of elimination. Unfortunately, this isn't necessarily the best practice. I urge you to evaluate yourselves accordingly. Ask yourself; What are the true intentions of my heart? And how can I use that to glorify God? Once the inventory is complete take what's good, use it, and leave what's not on the altar in repentance.

Dear God Almighty,

Forgive me for I have sinned. I asked that you will take hold of the reins to my mind so that I may be forgiven. Bless my mind, body and soul as I search for you throughout the day today. Remove anything within me that is unlike you and replace it with love,

power, and a sound mind. In Jesus' (Yahshua) most precious name.
    Amen

(These pages are inserts from C. Sims personal Journal)

CHAPTER 7

Nothing to Hide

Going from glory to glory is a lifelong commitment. One must be willing to do some much-needed self-reflection through transparency and truth to determine who they truly are. Facing the ugly parts within us could make this difficult. The unpacking of our baggage is necessary and essential for our growth to even begin. Laying down our lives to pick up the life that God intended for us starts with pouring all that we are ashamed of; out and sorting through the debris. We can overcome anything through the truth of our testimonies (Revelations 12:11). God takes our testimonies as a living sacrifice and burns them at the altar. In this fair exchange, we are given beauty for ashes (Isaiah 61:3). Jesus promises that if we give it over to him, in return we will have everlasting abundant life (1 Corinthians 3:11-15).

As I watch the sunset on the hills of Blooming Grove, NY, I am overwhelmed with peace and joy. I stand tall, holding myself accountable for who I have become. I found myself chasing things to fill the void. Things that would add nothing to it nor fulfill it. I was seeking attention, trying to find my place of relevance through fake love and imaginary relationships.

People who are raised in a hostile environment often learn how to live in survival mode while those who are raised in loving nurturing environments learn how to live in a healthy state of being. Both situations shape how we operate in our daily lives. This is why some are able to adapt while others fall short. However, there is hope for all if one just reaches out one's hand. We all gain opportunities that intend on leading us to Christ in one way or another.

For me, this has been such a hard process. I actually am not sure how to continue but I will go on being transparent while serving God, while being content and faithful in my own life. I am scared but knowing God is my strength allows me to keep on. God knows we have fears, but we cannot let it deter us. With God, I am strong therefore, his strength lends me the power to complete this task he has set before me. In finishing this manuscript it is my hope that someone will find value in this. I know that telling my side of the story will not only set me free but will also provide someone the opportunity to learn from my mistakes.

My fear of being exposed left me empty and broken through the majority of my adult life. I say this not for pity but as a matter of fact. Not wanting this led me to hide away but it has been long overdue. I needed to find my freedom and let it ring through my heart. My hope is to share these ugly painful truths and cast it into the swine so they drown in the brook of life. "We are of

God. He who knows God hears us, he who is not of God does not hear us. By this, we know the spirit of truth and the spirit of error." (1 John 4:6).

Through deliverance, I was liberated and set free. But it started with me being transparent with myself and then asking God to partner with me on my own rescue mission. Repentance can be hard to do because one must whole-heartedly face themselves at the door of forgiveness first. Asking God to throw your sins into the sea of forgetfulness starts with you offering it all to him.

1 Corinthians (10:12) states, "Therefore let him who thinks he stands take heed lest he fall. No temptation has overtaken you except such as is common to man; but God is faithful, who will not allow you to be tempted beyond what you are able but with the temptation will also make a way of escape, that you may be able to bear it."

"Be sober, be vigilant; because your adversary the devil, as a roaring lion, walketh about, seeking whom he may devour: Whom resist steadfast in the faith...." (1 Peter 5:8-9).

Everything happens for a reason. It could either teach us something, to urge us to educate ourselves and others, or help open ourselves up to something different. For many, this healing process differs. We often search this world only to find there's nothing to be found here for we're looking outside of ourselves. It's the inner spirit that we seek but having no knowledge of it brings us to places we can't recover from, even with help.

The enemy knew who I was long before I had a chance to find myself. It's the only explanation I have for the life-changing events that I experienced. But nevertheless, we all know that the plans of the adversary are spoiled by the covering of the blood of Jesus Christ. Take a moment to visit the little girl in me.

I was introduced to sex at a very early age. As a teenager I became promiscuous but hide it very well. I didn't want the secret of my abuse to be discovered by anyone nor did I want to be blamed for what I was later indulging in. The things that I hid were well-taught, owing to my experiences as a child. It begin at the age of five when a man, who was at that time a friend of the family forced himself on me. He started touching me while I was asleep. It became something I expected to happen every time I visited my grandmother's home. I learned how to pretend to be asleep as I laid on the bed, waiting for him to come into the room. I was literally frozen, stiff in fear during the act. I related to the movie 'The Color Purple' where Sophia stated, "a girl child is not safe in a house of men". Being unprotected at that age caused me to dislike who I was inside and out. I recall trying to tell my momma on two separate occasions. Once when it was happening and the other, when I was a preteen. Each time went undocumented because I was incapable of articulating what actually happened. It was a struggle for trying to even talk about it paralyzed me. I decided to cope by being very quiet. I was the epitome of 'how to be seen and not heard'. It was then that I learned how to fade into the background. I didn't even cry during that time. I didn't have emotions; I was just numb as I sucked my thumb.

Many children never report their abuse in fear of being blamed. This fear comes from their own misdirected guilt, shame, and confusion of what has happened to them. When a child has been sexually abused, they often become stagnant in their psychological development. It's as if their mind is unable to move past the violation. God forbid it happens multiple times over the course of their lives. It's not as easy as saying, "get over it". Sex is now a part of their growth so it manifests itself in ways that is unnatural.

I thought about it a lot as I sat in silence during the early stage of my life post the abuse. I often replayed things that happened over and over in my head trying to figure out what I did to cause it. I remember my grandmother's efforts to get me out of my thoughts during that time by teaching me how to bake, cook, and garden among other creative things. As a caregiver of a child who has been sexually abused, one must first be aware of the behavioral changes in their child. Then create a safe space for open communication with their child. And educate themselves on child abuse. This will help foster a conducive environment for healing from the abuse.

I began searching for validation in everything I did as I grew up. Looking for approval in areas of my life where I didn't need approval from others. Always wanting to be a part of a group but not really knowing how to fit in. I grew into my awkward shyness which led me to my love for reading. Books were my means of escape. I would soon learn how to socialize through the pages of the books I read. In school, I was a good model student who had a small circle of friends. One weekend, my mom allowed me to spend the night at a friend's house. My first overnight stay at someone's house who was not family became my last when my mom was called to come pick me up because I locked myself in the bathroom after my friend's uncle put his hand up my dress while I was at the kitchen table eating. All I remember was I was happy to get the big piece of chicken and I wanted to take my time and savor each bite. So, I was left in the kitchen alone after everyone else had finished eating. The uncle came in to get something to drink and sat down next to me. He whispered to me, "be still". I actually thought there was a bee or fly on me and he was going to kill it. But when I felt his hand touch my thigh, I immediately jumped up and ran into the bathroom. My friend was the only one I would let in. I told her to have her mom call my mom. She insisted on me telling her what happened so I did. She then said, "oh, he does that to me all the time." I was yelling at this point so somebody would call my mom. It took my mother to come to the bathroom to get me so I would come out. On the drive home, we did not talk at all. When we got home, my uncle and dad asked me what happened. I was reluctant to tell them because I didn't want anyone to get in trouble, mainly me. But my dad assured me it was not my fault and that he was a bad man. My mom called my friend's mother after I told them what she had said to me. Needless to say, that was the end of that friendship.

As a child, I feared everything and trusted no one. I stayed close to home, played alone mostly, and had a million thoughts, too many for a child. I would pray and ask Jesus to help me with everything. I often felt that I was a disappointment to my mother so I pretended a lot back then. I never wanted to be the reason my momma was unhappy. I made it a point to laugh and smile with her often. I used her to mask the pain I was feeling within myself. As a teenager, I began to be noticed by grown men. They would stare, some even approached me. I liked the attention I must admit. I found myself playing shy and flirting at the same time. One man in particular was the one I was willing to give myself to. He was the one I would defy my mother's rules for. He would be the one whom I would sneak in through the back door when no one was home. He only touched me with his hands but he was the man who would help open me up to the many others that followed.

My first boyfriend was someone I actually offered myself to, completely. Silly me, I foolishly thought he and I would be together forever. I can honestly say I loved him. I was content with him. But then something happened. I was raped by my best friend's boyfriend. He was clever in his approach. He gave me a ride home and asked if he could use the bathroom. I had a sense of security and believed he would never hurt me. He ended up forcing himself on me and made me take a bath afterwards. He also called my boyfriend's brother to tell him what had happened. But his version of what had taken place was much different than mine of course. I didn't know what was going on or why he felt the need to tell anyone at the time. But later, it was clear and clearer today when I think about how that particular incident revealed it all. How my best friend had already formed a disdained hatred towards me. The events that took place after that led me into deep depression followed by a downward spiral of uncontrollable urges. I found myself breaking it off with my boyfriend mostly due to guilt. I was also too ashamed to tell anyone what happened but I managed to confide in one person. A friend who I believe unto this day has never mentioned it to anyone.

These ugly events led me to a prolonged period of darkness in my life. However, if it were not for these circumstances, I don't believe I would ever know what true love really was. Sometimes, we go through things not for our own growth but also for the growth of those who will someday benefit from what we learned. The take away is that through it all, Jesus covers us in our sins and loves us unconditionally back to a place in the sun where no shadow can overtake us. The enemy would like us to believe there is no hope for us when we have fallen short in areas of adultery, sexual immortality, or any other sin. It is his duty to steal our hope, kill our aspirations, and destroy our future but he is a liar and a defeated foe in who has no power over us (John 10:10, 12:31, 16:11).

Child abuse is, I believe a generational curse that has never been dealt with properly and broken from one generation to the next. It has perpetrated itself here in the United States into what is now a 50-billion-dollar industry known as sex trafficking. Children are being sold all over as sex slaves. There are organized government task forces designed to fight against these organizations, raise awareness, and provide safe havens for children who have been trafficked. These teams continue to make strides in their efforts. However, due to the growing demand of child sex slaves, this is a never-ending battle. Many Americans are oblivious to this even happening in their own backyard. They believe that this is an issue that happens in other countries and not here, which is not at all true. The most interesting fact of all is that the business of child trafficking is increasingly growing. Some may ask the question, "Who are these people looking to buy children? And why isn't anyone reporting these people to the authorities?". The answer to these questions will blow your mind even more.

That then? Shall we sin because we are not under the law but under grace? By no means! Don't you know that when you offer yourself to someone as obedient slaves, you are slaves of the one you obey- whether you are slaves to sin, which leads to death, or to obedience, which leads to righteousness? But thanks be to God that, though you used to be slaves to sin, you have come to obey from your heart the pattern of teaching that has now claimed your allegiance. You have been set free from sin and have become slaves to righteousness.

(Romans 6:15-18)

Doing the same thing over and over again expecting a different result is insanity. We definitely can't keep sinning and think our lives will change for the better. No, the wage of sin is death. It's not a physical death but a spiritual death. People are pleasing their every desire, expecting to live a life of indulgence. But where does it leave us? When we've had our share of folly and we've exposed ourselves in so many ways, what is left? God simply asks that we repeat (confess what's wrong) and he will make crooked places straight.

Dear LORD my Father,

Thank you for saving me from myself. Thank you for making crooked places straight in my life. Thank you for stretching out your hand towards me so I could hold on to you. Father, touch my body, mind, and soul. Renew me from the crown on my head to the soles of my feet. Make everywhere my feet tread my territory to claim. In Jesus' (Yahshua) name.

Amen.

(These pages are inserts from C. Sims personal Journal)

CHAPTER 8

You Can't Have Your Cake & Eat it Too!

By the time I met my husband, I was tired of being involved with the familiar sexual spirits I found in other men. I wanted to settle, or settle down as they called it. I can honestly say I used my husband when we began dating. I used him to get over the one I was truly in love with. I didn't intend for our relationship to last as long as it did. Four years of dating and a baby later, he asked me to marry him. I said yes because he was my child's father and I had grown to love him in so many ways. I was all in before our wedding. I was busy ignoring all the signs, the red flags, to care about what was really going on behind the scenes. A month before our wedding, I found out we were expecting another child. It was not what I had planned but it was our reality.

Once married, I understood the reality of compatibility. Neither my husband or I was interested in one another the relationship became more of a routine. The affection that once was present had died. He was well aware that I was a spoiled brat but I felt I needed his attention as a form of validation. I craved him more as we became more distance from one another. My idea of marriage involved having free sex as much as possible. This definitely was not the case, and it left me feeling empty inside. I was not really sure what was happening to our relationship. He desired to go out more, leaving me home. I desired to be touched more than he cared to touch me. Those old tenancies became stronger and increased after I was forced into isolation post the birth of my second child. My husband was a devoted father nevertheless, he was unfaithful to say the least.

From doing everything together, he shifted to staying out until later, sometimes not even making it back home. I justified his actions by concluding that he needed some male comradery, as many men do, once a week after working so hard. But no matter how I justified it, nothing stopped me from feeling unwanted by the one that once desired me. I concluded I had to weigh my options on how to fill this void I was feeling; I decided by going out once a week as well maybe I would have some fulfillment. I didn't think it through at all. I just kept pretending. In essences lying to myself and my husband. My grandmother used to say, " I can't stand a liar. If you'll lie, you'll cheat, if you'll cheat, you'll steal, and if you'll steal, I don't want you nowhere around me." This very description was who I had become.

Be careful what you ask God for in your prayers because you just might get it. All I wanted was free sex. This concept baffles some and those that know, well they know. I recall, 2 Corinthians (4:8), "We are hard pressed on every side, yet not crushed; we are perplexed but not in despair". I didn't care about being right in my life, let alone in my marriage at the time. My focus was not on the right thing and I lived through it to tell the story of how on can think they are doing the right thing while actually doing the opposite. Our flesh is a powerful entity and I thank God that the spirit once fed is stronger.

When there is even a desire to do what is right, God can work with that. He leads, guides, and directs us through series of circumstances to get us to the very place he wishes us to be, in him, using all that we go through; to attain his blessings. It is true that everything happens for a reason. What we have in us determines the experiences we have to endure. But rest assured, God is with us. I am so grateful for the Holy spirit which resides inside of me. Only through Christ was I able to free myself from the enemy within. God always delivers us out of the hands of our enemies, we just have to be persistent in this walk of life to see the light at the end of the tunnel.

The spirit identifies with the spirit. I am grateful for those assigned to me. They are the ones that God has chosen to be my partners in prayer. The ones that continue to lift me up in prayer even when I don't hear from them in weeks, months or years. The ones who, through their obedience to God, unaware of what exactly is happening in my life; will pray for me when my name comes up in their spirit. These prayer warriors offer me strength even when I am unaware. They ask for nothing but in return, are given everything by the Lord. They are the ones who call at the drop of a dime just to encourage me while giving no thought to how they would gain anything from it. They prove that the spirit of the living God is powerful and mighty.

"Hello Christine, I am calling as I got free for a moment, I've been so busy lately." She said through the Bluetooth speakers of the car. "I just felt you in my spirit and wanted to let you know that you have been such an inspiration in my life since the very moment I met you." She continued. "Please don't get discouraged at this hour. I am not sure what's going on with you but know that

God is on your side and he will most definitely see you through. Be encouraged Sweetie, I love you but I have to go." Just like that God will speak to you through someone else.

She would never know what that two-to-three-minute phone call did for me in that exact moment. I would never share with her that I was driving and pleading with God to show up. I felt like I was falling apart in that instant. She would never ask what I was dealing with at the time. She was only carrying out God's work. She was being a friend in Jesus through her obedience. I pulled my car over to the side of the road and I cried like a baby. The thought that God would love me so always brings me to tears. However, there was something different about my crying this time. It allowed me to break free of the thoughts that were pegging me in that moment. It was the release I needed to course through the situation I found myself in at the time.

The thing about God is, he never leaves us comfortless. He has given us the Holy Spirit which resides within us (1 Corinthians 2:11). The spirit identifies with the spirit so it isn't strange that a three-minute phone call is all that's needed to assist you through a season of lacking or an hour of despair. During that time, I was seeking answers for my situation. I demanded that God hear my cry because his word in 1 Peter (5:7) told me that, "He cares for me." I was angry and was bold enough to express my anger in my plea to him. My God chose to show up in a personal way to show me that he most definitely heard my cry and that he was true to his word. There is always a lamb in the bush for those of us who seek our counsel from the Lord.

There is always a reason why we endure certain situations in our life. Sometimes it is to work something in or out of us but many times that reason has nothing to do with you per se but is designed specifically for you to help someone else along the way.

This is why Paul reminds us to rejoice (Romans 5) in our tribulations for two reasons—because we already have the victory over the situation through Christ Jesus and because others need to know that they can make it as well. We are truly overcomers by the word of our testimony (Revelations 12:11). These things are meant to be shared and never hidden. We are not to be ashamed of our past faults and failures. Even in them, everything happens for a reason.

The reason may not be clear at the moment but Romans (5:1-5) gives us food for thought as we continue on.

My daughter once shared in a radio interview; how she dealt with the injustice of being bullied during middle school. Being bullied made her extremely depressed. She even had suicidal thoughts. She stated that during the time, she remembered going to church one Sunday and her pastor said, "Everything happens for a reason, and God will not put more on us than we can bear (1 Corinthians 10:13). She admitted she could not understand why this was happening to her but she was crazy enough to endure it just to see what this pain she felt could possibly produce in her. For a child to grasp the concept of endurance in order to gain hope and character in the process is encouraging within itself. She gave me a sense of hope in that moment as well as others. This is what Jesus does. He provides us with a glimmer of hope to carry on to see what the end is going to look like. The enemy is assigned his position, whether we provoke him or not, he has an assignment of his own and he will do whatever he needs to do in order to test our faith. In Luke (22:31), Jesus informs Simon

Peter of Satan's task to sift each of us like wheat. I am so grateful that Jesus prayed for our faith to not fail us. That we understand that only for a season are we tested and after we have suffered a short time, we will stand in victory before others and testify on how we overcame it. Therefore, be encouraged when you are persecuted because you are not abandoned (2 Corinthians 4: 7-9). The building of our faith may need for things to be shaken up in our lives but that doesn't mean it will not pass.

But he said to me, "My grace is sufficient for you, for my power is made perfect in weakness." Therefore, I will boast all the more gladly about my weakness, in insults, in hardships, in persecutions, in difficulties. For when I am weak, then I am strong. I have made a fool of myself, but you drove me to it. I ought to have been commended by you, for I am not in the least inferior to the "super-apostles," even though I am nothing.

(2 Corinthians 12: 9-11)

Without God, we are equivalent to nothing. But with God we are more than conquerors. For everything that's lacking in us, God has provided to us. When we are lonely, God gives companionship. When we are hurt, he offers healing. When we are sad, he brings his joy. God is never going to bring the burden without covering that burden with his grace. We have to only believe and not give up. The night is darkest just before the break of day. We might as well hold on and see what the end's going to be.

Dear LORD my God, Almighty Creator and Father,

*   Thank you for victory over the things that try to tear me down. Where I am weak, you make me strong. My strength comes directly from you. Deliver me from*

the snares of my enemy. Build me up again I ask, in your son Jesus' (Yahshua)name I pray. Amen.

(These pages are inserts from
C. Sims personal Journal)

CHAPTER 9

Inside These Walls

The mind is a very powerful muscle. It can create small thoughts, multiply and magnify them. Whatever one sows in the garden of his mind, he also reaps that very thing. We are to consistently, no matter what is happening around us, think on those things that are good and offer perfection.

With all that is happening within the world today, people are less careful of those things that capture their eyes, ears and what often times, come out of their mouths. We all have been held victim by our own curse. We choose not to see it for what it is. Instead, we research plots and schemes while forming our own conspiracy theories for our situations. Putting names of people with faces and relationships so as to tie it to the stories as we go.

All too often, we do not consider the higher entity at hand. Speaking life into a dead situation does one thing and one thing only, it breathes life. Job tells us this, "For there is hope for a tree: If it is cut down, it will sprout again, and its tender shoots will not fail. If its roots grow old in the ground and its stump dies in the soil, at the scent of water, it will bud and put forth twigs like a sapling."

Being so far from home left me feeling isolated from what I held dear to my heart. I could not find my way back to God on my own. I did not feel the need to pray at all. I was falling deep into depression and the nightmares that I had of lions eating my flesh still shudders my spirit. If you ever felt lost within yourself, then you know what I mean.

One thing I learned during these dark moments is that God always protects those he loves. My auntie called me one morning. I answered the phone in the middle of an ugly cry. She immediately began to pray. Then she told me to read my bible, I cried even louder. It was hearing her voice on the phone that saved me from myself. She interceded by standing in the gap that was becoming increasingly widened through my lack of faith. She was my angel on earth during a time when I couldn't settle on my faith in Christ. She reassured me she was only a phone call away but I never called her. Instead, she called me daily to pray and to read the word of God. She took on the assignment to be the gardener as I was at that time, a delicate flower needing to be nurtured.

Sometimes, you just need a safe space

to lay your head while you think of nothing. Sometimes, you just need to be free to engage and free to withdraw from all the things of the world. Providing that space for another can seem taxing for some. But for those that understand, they get the importance of the need to just be. Waking up to the demands of life can be overwhelming when you have so much weighing on your heart. Those that keep pushing themselves to just go and be apart will soon find themselves breaking at the seams. But for those fortunate enough to have a place of serenity and loved ones who nurture us back are truly blessed.

The story of the gardener and the flower says it best. Someone must be the gardener, and someone must be the flower. Throughout life, you may find that the roles will switch from time to time, but the truth remains. When you are the gardener, you take on the responsibility of the flower's short comings until it buds for itself. Allowing the flower to be delicate and fragile in a place of comfort. When we do not understand this concept, life teaches it to us through our own experiences. Opening us up to situations that show us the gardener who undertakes the responsibility to nurture us. The fundability of its texture and how it depends on others.

Through this concept of giving ourselves, we are taught that in time, we need to retreat from the outside in to center ourselves and to be free of day-to-day tasks and concerns. Allowing a moment to reorganize gives strength to those who take on the burden of nurturing. This person, through sheer kindness or experience knows the importance of footing and timing. Being one with each other is key to building this relationship.

When we offer ourselves, there is a chance that we can be taken advantage of, however, there is also a higher chance that they will be rewarding accordingly. The heart's intention determines the outcome. If we are wishing to gain from our action of assisting others, we genuinely gain nothing. But if our hearts are pure in wishing to gain nothing, only to help, we gain everything. (Proverbs 4:23). A pure heart is key to success.

Things that are broken can often be used to create beautiful things when handled by a creative artist. The breath of life awakens the soul and rejuvenates what was once dormant. It takes great care to revive something from its old self, transforming it to something new and vibrant. Even the break of day has to come to a time of darkness, to emerge. However, as we bask in the sunshine of the light of day, we often times do not think of the night that will come soon as there are not enough hours in the day to do it all, leaving us onto a race focused on ticking each task from our to-do list. There is truly a time for everything.

Our lessons in life are personally designed based on the intentions of our heart. They are written solely on the intentions of our hearts and the thoughts in our minds. What we ponder determines what we get in life. Thoughts of ill intent leads you to failure. Thoughts of love and concern for other people besides yourself, will grant you provisions everywhere you go. Good thoughts breed good outcomes, even when the outcome is least expected, the thought of it being a good one pushes it to succeed.

When we cultivate our relationship with Jesus, we allow for our will to be connected to his will. We are walking hand in hand with him. We are intrigued by his wisdom and knowledge. Like all marriages, if we are not walking as one there is no way for it to stand. Standing on the

LORD's strong foundation offers true loving power. Spending time becomes more than just QT (quality time), it becomes an unbreakable bond that strengthens over time. One must be diligent in seeking opportunities to spend time with Jesus in the presence of the Holy Spirit. One must be vigilant in guarding their heart from anything that exhausts itself over the Lord, our God. One must also have a heart of compassion, knowing that they too were covered in spots and blemishes once upon a time but are now, set free.

The battle ground of the mind seeks to have its way stray away from the will of God. However, it is our duty to take every thought captive, compare it to the word of God, then ask the comforter for direction.

By tampering with the minds of the African slaves, our forefathers cursed themselves in two parts through the very word of God they used to justify their wrongdoings. The word says, "Touch not my anointed and do my prophet no harm". Many feel this is directed towards a specific group of people however, God is speaking of his chosen people way before groups or titles were a thing. Secondly, "touch not the mind".

When God tells us to meditate on the word,

he is telling us to think on it, analyze it, bring it under submission of our understanding. We are in no way, shape or form be willing to allow our minds to be altered. Colossians (2:8) states, "See to it that no one takes you captive by philosophy and empty deceit, according to human tradition, according to the elemental spirits of the world, and not according to Christ."

"Confess and renounce this sin and activity before God, the Father. Take away the legal right for this demon to stay attached to you. Verbally speak to it and tell it has no place in your life and it has to go. In the mighty name of Yahshua who is Christ Jesus. Breaking the curse from these things will drop the scales from our eyes and allow the Holy Spirit to rest, rule and abide in us once more. This is the individual work that must be done in our homes to heal the land." (James 4:6-7)

"God gives us specific instructions to take on the truth of the word however, in doing so we must be changed from our former selves. We no longer have free rein to those things that may have caused us to sin. We are now new creatures." (Ephesians 4: 20 -24)

I am pleased to add, as a witness through my

own testimony that God's grace is so sufficient that any entity that has held you captive can be cast out immediately in the name of Jesus. This power of authority is given to all who believe it. Once we truly come to God with our sins, his saving grace heals and sets us free. The widespread liberation of people is not written in the constitution in fact, it is written in the word of God.

Many people have tried everything else. They have opened themselves up to hypnosis and fortune tellers, they have yet to come to the realization that they have been turned over to a reprobated mind. But the good news is that there is no condemnation for those who are now in Christ Jesus. We all need a little more Jesus, as the song goes. If we turn towards the love of Christ, we are freed from the tricks and schemes of our enemy. Our oppressors no longer have power over us.

I once found myself as a part of a cult. This congregation thrived from the foundation of intimidation and manipulation. Its bullying techniques were clearly used to oppress those who were involved. Cults are usually created to cover the sins of its leaders. The spirit of Delila was evident in that these people who slow walked you into their charms. It was a process. Our minds have a way of coming under submission through a repetitive state. Many times, we are not aware of what it is until we are completely removed from the situation. But once we are fully cognitive of this, we can remove the hold that the adversary has over us.

Asking God to remove it by confessing it and then giving him full authority over that thing, then commanding that it be removed in Jesus' name is the only thing that will release its hold over us. The story of how king Nebuchadnezzar lost his mind for a period of time but was restored back to his throne comes to mind. In the book of Daniel, you can find that Nebuchadnezzar summons Daniel to interpret a dream that he had. Turns out the dream became a reality for the king. We sometimes must live out a situation for us to truly surrender to God completely. Through our own free will, we experience what we seek even if it is not good for us.

How would a child know the stove is hot lest he touches it and learns? I used to believe that pain will help you remember and in most cases it does however, this is not God's wish for his children.

God wants us to come to the full understanding of who we are; but more importantly who we are in him. Only through the Holy Spirit will we be able to accomplish this.

My goal is that they may be encouraged in heart and united in love, so that they may have the full riches of complete understanding, in order that they may know the mystery of God, namely, Christ.

                                      (Colossians 2:2)

Having a full understanding that God's perfect timing and plans supersede our own is what faith looks like. We all have mile stones that we wish to accomplish in our lives. Sometimes, our plans don't always coincide with the ones God has in store. Keep in mind, the delay doesn't necessarily mean rejection. It simply means not yet. Some of our hearts' desire requires growth. It's better to praise while going through the waiting period than to complain, "why me". We can trust that it will work out in our favor.

Dear Lord,

    Search my heart through and through. If you find anything that is unlike you, prune it away. As I go about my day, remind me of your promises. Cover me in the blood of Jesus from the crown on my head to the soles of my feet. Keep me safe from all hurt, harm, and pain. In Jesus' (Yahshua) name, I pray.

    AMEN

      (These pages are inserts from C. Sims personal Journal)

CHAPTER 10

The Sweet Spot

Joseph's brothers threw him into a pit and sold him into slavery as the result of envy and jealousy (Genesis 37:2-36). They did not expect him to be the one who would save them from death during a famine. The one that got away to save the others was first abandoned by those he trusted and cared for. Many of us who have been mishandled and left alone often find an area of solace that not only allows us to be rediscovered but also provides a way out that we never could imagine. I too, was left to face this world alone after being rejected by those I love, but my gifts made room for me (Proverbs 18:16). King Jesus saw something he could use in me. The analytical side of my brain would force me to inquire of God what man could not provide. This led me to journaling a lot more than usual. My writing has been all I've had to show for what I've been through and I was saving it for a time like this.

God saw fit to shut me off from the outside world for a time period with no one to talk to. I was forced into isolation because my own fears held me there. I had little to no trust in people after all that I had seen during this time. The evils of this world are great. Even when your intentions are good, you can still end up being wrong. As I sit in my mountain cottage, just before the break of day, I think about how I have been set aside for the purpose of being cultivated and shaped into the woman I always wanted to be. God will indeed make crooked places straight and I am a living testimony of that fact.

Speaking to my best friend, I mentioned I wanted to be a motivational speaker. She said, "Really?" then laughed and asked "what would you speak on?" When I replied, "Love" she looked at me straight in the face and said, "What do you know about love, Renee?" in such a condescending tone as if I knew nothing at all. Her statement made me pause in that moment. I immediately asked the Holy Spirit to reveal her to me. We've been friends for over thirty years. I never knew she didn't really know me at all. However, there were obvious signs revealed over time. Asking God to reveal things about this friendship opened a door to secrets that would end up changing me for the rest of my life.

Love doesn't dissolve over time, it doesn't remove itself when the truth of betrayal, drama, or devastation is cast over you. Love is what repairs and amends. The heart aches while love lingers around to mend the broken-hearted. Love has no expiration date, it stays long after the hurt has dwindled, it even heals the pain of the betrayal, then blossoms into a new season. Those who believe love hurts, mistake love for other things because of the circumstances they fall victim to. Most confuse love with loneliness, rejection, envy, jealousy etc. but the reality is love is everywhere. Love never hurts. Looking back now, I realize my bff was absolutely correct. I knew nothing about love, well not this love. She in fact, knew the old me long enough to know I was selfish and sometimes heartless but she didn't realize how I was being purged of the things I used to be when we knew one another, at the time. Back then, everything I knew about love was a lie. However, the journey to true love began without me even being aware of it.

The love of Jesus is greater than any love I've ever experienced. A friend that loves you, pushes you to greatness, sits in the dirt with you during your darkest hour, allows you to break down and then assists you in rebuilding your confidence. The love of Jesus is a phenomenon every man, woman, and child should have access to. He acknowledges all your faults and loves you for who you are. This love sees your naked truth and protects you. This love stays even when your sins are exposed. This love knows no boundaries or limits on how far it will go for you. This love will fight for you. The love of Jesus is the only love you will ever need; once received. It fills voids, supplies things you lack in, and keeps secrets. This love doesn't falter when you call it quits, it stays true even when you don't. Closer than a brother or a friend, there is no greater love than that of Jesus (Proverbs 18:24, John 15:13). This is what I found love to be.

Sitting in my driveway after a family vacation, my life took a devastating turn in a matter of minutes. As I tried to pull myself together after my husband told me he was unhappy and was leaving, I prayed to the Lord asking him to show me that I am still lovable. I don't think I was ever fully prepared for what that prayer would manifest. In my mind, my husband had just told me he no longer loved me. I would later learn that, that was definitely not true. He did love me but he could no longer dwell with me. He'd had enough. I must admit I could not deal with me either back then. I had been angry for far too long. Still, I was crying as if I had done nothing wrong. I could have taken all the blame for what our marriage had become but instead I chose to point the finger and not suffer through my own guilt. He wasn't happy because he found out, ironically, through mere pillow talk with his mistress that he wasn't the only one having an affair. He wanted to leave because he needed to prove to her that he was not invested at all. I gave them both what they needed. I owned the dramatic devastation because I wanted others to believe I was distraught by him leaving. When really, I was relieved. He had taken care of me and our two children. He had seen me get through college both times. He had stayed put while I got myself together financially. We had both been unhappy for years but we kept trying to force our square peg into a round hole. As I found my way into the bitterness, I began to think of all those things I wanted that he wouldn't allow me to have. Facing a new challenge, I set my sight on those things. But nothing really seemed to work. It wasn't long before I was back to square one.

This journey of craving self-satisfaction led me to this 700 square feet cottage in the mountains, alone, awaiting what happens next. I had been preparing for quarantine all my life.

Growing up as an only child taught me how to be alone. It never really bothered me to go to places by myself or be my own company. I actually prefer it to having to deal with a group-like situation. Some people call me an introvert or a loner, I just call it "being me". Forcing myself to be a part of something has never been me. As soon as it was not clear where I stood in the lives of others, I would simply remove myself. It wasn't worth my time to figure out anything. When things became fussy, I just took them as a sign. I felt my heart was safe that way. I spent twenty-five years holding on to something that was not worth it, therefore I decided that nothing else would get that privilege. So now, here I am thinking of those I've celebrated and prayed for; who have gone on to reap what they have sowed. I, on the other hand, am waiting for the harvest of what I have sown to ripen so as to lay my anger, bitterness, lust and fear to rest forever. I believe my enemies want me to give up. Nevertheless, that is not my fate. I shall not die but declare the works of the Lord (Psalms 118:17).

The time for me to be still came just as all hell was breaking loose on earth, owing to this pandemic. I was placed in an area where the

Covid-19 virus was running rampant. The state of New York was hit the hardest in the United States, during the early stages of this virus' discovery. However, right before the outbreak of the virus was announced on the daily news, I was hit with my own dilemma. I had been placed on administrative leave pending an investigation on my current position, which later resulted in my termination. To my surprise, I was thankful when my supervisor called to tell me I was fired. She informed me that the investigation proved I had falsified documents, the very ones that she had trained and authorized me on. I was extremely happy with the results and the feeling was conveyed over the phone. She paused for a moment before asking me if I had heard her correctly. I asked if she could repeat it for clarity. She was delighted to oblige so she repeated exactly what she said before but in a pleasing tone. I smiled as I responded, "Oh yes, I heard you quite clearly, thank you for calling." I was happy, she was happy, it all worked out for the both of us I suppose. She kept at the conversation by asking me what I wish to do with the items left on my desk. I told her they were of no value and she could throw away anything she had found. I thanked her for calling and proceeded to hang up. I am not sure why she felt the need to prolong the conversation but we continued on as she wanted to be sure I understood what was happening. I was fired, what's not clear about that. I reassured her. I knew precisely what 'being terminated' meant and wished her well.

Being on administrative leave, all of this took place because I was in the wrong place at the wrong time and was witness to a conversation I was never supposed to hear, at all. My supervisor asked me to come into the office to recant a written statement I made on my coworker, Cathy's behalf. However, I refused and chose to support Cathy by telling the truth in a matter that would put my supervisor under investigation. Andrea chose to suspend me. Falsifying documentations was the basis of my suspension. My schedule verified that I should have been with a client at the time of the conversation. However, upon finishing one visit, I realized I had not packed the application for my next scheduled home visit therefore, I went back to the office to retrieve it. En route, I contacted my client to inform him I would be late. This was not unusual as I always allotted time for unforeseen issues during visits, as suggested by my trainer, supervisor. During several supervisions, I was told that I must always align my scheduled appointments with the documented notes for each client. "To make sure everything matches", she said.

Andrea Nanez took on her first leadership role during a trying time in her own personal life. Being formally rejected, bullied, abandoned, and full of anxiety, she was determined to push through it all. She was very ambitious and wanted to succeed at her newly appointed role. She embodied the preconceptions of the leaders she admired within her field. She wanted to be seen as authoritative and strong instead of how she really felt, the total opposite. Standing five feet and five inches from the ground, she felt like she was finally being heard as she demanded total silence and eye contact during staff meetings. It was obvious she was growing a little taller each day through her position. Facing four strong-willed black women, many who outnumbered her in age was beginning to be a challenge. These women had their own ideas, corporate experiences and education that they all brought to the table. However, this seemed to intimidate Andrea in some way. Being accused of speaking out of turn

Christian Reborn 141

in a moment of true revelation on who she really was as a person, it was time to get tough. She had manipulated others and used her privilege among other things to gain this position and was willing to do anything at this point to salvage her reputation. The idea of a simple educated black woman taking away what she had built in her career with one allegation was asinine. As I said, I simply was in the wrong place at the wrong time and heard something that was not intended for me to hear, let alone repeat it as a witness for my coworker.

Nevertheless, I was happy to not go back to work. Those two weeks of reflection led me to the conclusion that I no longer wanted to go into a place where I had to put on a pretentious face or boost the self-esteem of people who had to puff themselves up because of their title. I had experienced this a lot more than I care to admit. I recalled Cookie telling me that my education and the way I carried myself threatened my supervisor. People who see me as intimidating have no idea of the insecurities, I carry within myself. They have no way of knowing that with the Bachelor's degree, came the battle of abuse and with the Master's degree, came a struggle of neglect. I was already beaten down and had nothing left in me to uphold but those certifications on that mere piece of paper called my resume, along with God who was the lifter of my head. So, there is nothing to be intimidated by, nothing at all.

I realized the enemy sees our light long before we do. No one saw the little girl sucking her thumb, rubbing her ear but instead, they saw who I was long before I was even aware. This is what Jesus does. He introduces us to others as he sees us, not how we see ourselves. I used to think that something was wrong with me. Why didn't I fit in with the groups and clichés I so desperately wanted to be a part of? Why was I so different? Why, even in my sin I was set apart? I would indulge in smoking cannabis and then go read my bible. I would sleep with one man after another and then go pray for repentance. This was just who I was or so I thought. I wasn't cognizant that my spirit was trying to override my flesh at the time. I was not conscious that this was the Holy Spirit pulling me to righteousness. This is the overwhelmingly reckless love of God.

I began to accept the opinions of others just so I could fit in but that didn't last long. My God-given nature eventually outweighed it all. God woke me up to who he wanted me to be. Without the noise and judgments of others, Jesus spoke to me directly despite what a previous pastor once told me, "God doesn't speak to us that way or that quickly."

I felt like I had been on an accelerated course in my relationship with the Lord because he spoke to me often and timely during our conversations. I dare not say this to the man of God however.

Faith is the substance of things hoped for and the evidence of things not seen (Hebrews 11:1). I often hope for things that may seem unrealistic to some. I've watched through the windows of my own eyes; how God has provided these things. I've hoped and it was revealed. Many times, there were desperate circumstances wherein I needed help. Other times, it was a simple case of longing.

For example, I was once pulled over by an officer of the Sheriff's department after smoking a blunt as I drove down the street. It was obviously something I could not hide so I elected to tell the truth when asked. He searched my car and found the contents as I described to him. Then proceeded to write me a ticket. This was marked as the worst day ever given the timing of the matter however, I hoped the outcome would result in nothing at all.

A month or so later, as I appeared in court to speak to the DA with regard to the charges that were set before me, I had faith that it would be fine. My nerves did not get the memo of course but my heart was comforted by a small voice of my dad saying, "it's going to be alright, Papie", the only nickname and the only person I would ever allow to call me anything other than my given name. And I emerged from the court room moments later, $250 short with a moving violation of parking near a fire hydrant. My brother in law's facial expression was priceless as he was also in attendance in the courtroom that day and had known the reason for me being there.

This is not taken lightly, and I do not seek to boost or brag but only to point out that in my most desperate moments, I chose to believe that all things will work out in my favor. This particular phenomenon has repeated many times throughout my life however, now that I am seasoned, I seek to encourage others to find trust, believe and hope in faith for then, you will always be unscathed. Is this some form of witchcraft or some sorcery? Well, of course not. It is the promise of our Lord, our creator, and savior.

We have all fallen short by forgetting who we truly are. It takes occasions and situations to remind us of who we are and whose, we are.

As Christians, we often proclaim to believe in things we constantly doubt. But when we stand on what we say and believe, the God within us shows up and shows out. We can walk in peace with no worry, no stress and trust that even the things that make us cry out in pain are working in our favor. It is true that it's already done.

So, what are those things that you concern yourselves with? List them if you need to. But once you have identified them all, make a conscious decision to give it to the Lord. I recommend putting that list in your bible. Then praise God for deliverance from it. When it comes back to mind, tell the adversary he is a liar and you have given them up to the Lord, it is done. Then praise the lord again.

The freedom of submission in faith will give you a confidence that can't be taken away. It will make you appear cocky to those who don't understand what it truly looks like to be fearfully and wonderfully made.

It took me to be around my siblings to really see myself for who I was and to accept who I had found within myself. The little idiosyncrasies I was criticized for, became clear to me while watching them as we all interacted with one another. Now that I was aware that I was not alone in my peculiars, God then took me to a secret place of isolation to heal from my brokenness and to teach me how to love myself. I became the paradigm of Psalm 91. This message of hope would stay rooted as I went through what I call a selfcare season. God separated me from the parts of myself I no longer needed. He freed me from my own self destruction, my enemy who was within me had to go. This is when I entered into the sweet spot, the enlightenment.

God has given us all the opportunity to fulfill the desires of our hearts. It is perfectly designed to create growth and development for all involved. When we learn who we are in Christ Jesus, we experience a depth of love that has never been tapped into. The reality is hard to believe but this is why we are peculiar people. Believing and trusting a higher power of authority that is in control of every aspect of our lives. How we move, prosper and grow. To some it may seem crazy but until they see God for who he is, they will never recognize the truth. God takes all the catastrophic situations in our lives to shape and mold us into better versions of ourselves in every way but only if we trust him. Most people believe there are other things they could be doing. And there are however, none of those things will bring balance to our lives. Once the foundation is made, growth can take place. Being open to the truth is liberating and freeing in a way that brings peace and substantial pleasure for life. In the sweet spot is where God wants all of us to be, resting in his hands where no matter where we tread, we have dominion.

When we wake with a higher consciousness of who we are and whose we are, we must stay in tune with everything that opened us up to evolve spiritually. It is more than spa visits and gym time. God has allowed me to tap into another side of myself. One where I have full access to my emotions and train of thought. Anything that threatens it—no matter how close or how invested, my body, mind and soul rejects it immediately. In this state of being, I have found myself to be at peace which is greatly resounding within my spirit.

CHAPTER 11

Amazing Grace

J ohn 17 (11-26) depicts the love Jesus has for all
of us. Upon Jesus' knowledge of his limited
presence on earth, he petitions the throne

of grace on our behalf, is inspiring and holds a degree of compiling obligation to us as children of Christ. The New International Version notes it like this:

> *11 I will remain in the world no longer, but they are still in the world, and I am coming to you. Holy Father protect them by the power of your name, the name you gave me, so that they may be one as we are one. 12 While I was with them, I protected them and kept them safe by that name you gave me. None has been lost except the one doomed to destruction so that Scripture would be fulfilled. 13 "I am coming to you now, but I say these things while I am still in the world, so that they may have the full measure of my joy within them. 14 I have given them your word and the world has hated them, for they are not of the world any more than I am of the world. 15 My prayer is not that you take them out of the world but that you protect them from the evil one. 16 They are not of the world, even as I am not of it. 17 Sanctify them by[c] the truth; your word is truth. 18 As you sent me into the world, I have sent them into the world. 19 For them*

I sanctify myself, that they too may be truly sanctified. 20 "My prayer is not for them alone. I pray also for those who will believe in me through their message, 21 that all of them may be one, Father, just as you are in me and I am in you. May they also be in us so that the world may believe that you have sent me. 22 I have given them the glory that you gave me, that they may be one as we are one— 23 I in them and you in me—so that they may be brought to complete unity. Then the world will know that you sent me and have loved them even as you have loved me. 24 "Father, I want those you have given me to be with me where I am, and to see my glory, the glory you have given me because you loved me before the creation of the world. 25 "Righteous Father, though the world does not know you, I know you, and they know that you have sent me. 26 I have made you[d] known to them, and will continue to make you known in order that the love you have for me may be in them and that I myself may be in them."

We never really stop wondering what happens next. This is evident in our planning, goal setting and daily conversations with one another. But our comfort comes with knowing that it has already been taken care of. The next chapter of our lives has already been written. God is truly the author and finisher of our faith. Learning how to maneuver through life, fully trusting Jesus is one task, once learned, we shall never forget. Easier than riding a bicycle for when we rely on our faith, our faith never fails us. Just like riding a bike however, there will be times when you stumble and even fall. Of course, we will make mistakes from time to time. It's not about the number of mistakes made. The thing that matters most is what we learned from those mistakes. What can be used for growth?

With time, consistency, and enough patience, you can teach old dogs, new tricks. Before long, you will reap the benefits of a job well done. Stay the course and grant yourself as well as others a little grace. It will be worth the effort. Not everyone will understand but when you have been approved by God, it won't matter what anyone thinks. They will become critical, even combative at times. Love them through it. Some will have to witness the glory of God's grace in your life for their own development.

Others will fall short without notice or care. Those who speak division and strife are merely bystanders but they too have a purpose in the process. Your job is to continue in love to show them something they may not have seen if they were not connected to you. Do not worry about the pessimists, nor the back-biters, just continue following God's designed plan for your life. It is the Lord that prepares the table, the enemy is invited to have a front row seat to witness his glory.

"It's not always tragedy that produces trauma.", Lizzo says to David Letterman in an episode of 'No introduction needed', a talk show on Netflix. This statement made a resounding impact on my spirit. Sometimes, it's as simple as the lack of reciprocation. We don't always get from others what we give and that's okay as long as we give, genuinely from the heart for our rewards will surpass our expectations.

I've had to learn several things on this journey of life. One being that my best may not look like anyone else's but it's mine and I own it. Another is my shortcomings have become opportunities to learn and develop and to glean from others. I came to understand that past experiences do not define who I am nor does it dictate my future.

There is this saying back in my hometown that starts many phone conversations it's "They say....". For instance, Chile, they say she pregnant by that woman's husband. Or They say, he was at the others woman's house. Or They say so and so died of a heart attack, I heard it was Aids at first. The gossip line goes 24/7 in Vicksburg, MS. It does not matter if it is truth or fact if "They Say" then it is so. As a little girl, I would hear my mother and her sisters' gossip on the phone regularly. I used to call them Channel 4, Channel 3, and Channel 5 news. I despise overhearing some of the foolishness. I asked my mom, "why do you repeat stuff like that?" I had an understanding incredibly early in life that if it does not honor or glorify, it diminishes and breaks down others. Repeating what others say and believing it only perpetuates the cruse of a slave mentality. Gossip is a learned behavior, operated by those who wish to know or be involved in things that have no value or premises. Gossip is known as casual or unconstrained conversation or reports about other people typically involving details that are not confirmed as being true. Gossip has been researched in terms of its origins in evolutionary psychology, which has found it to be an important means for people to monitor cooperative reputations and so, maintain widespread indirect reciprocity. (Wikipedia)

They say I think I am all that, smarter, beautiful, and better than, but God said I am his. They don't see the insecure, frightened little girl who often visits her grandma's kitchen table clutching the wooden bowl and spoon fixing her face while trying to hold back tears of regret, wondering how her safe space was violated. They don't see the dark spots from the open wounds that secrete fluids of itchy serum as the scars heal. What they see and misinterpret as strength is only covered through weakness in Christ. I most certainly do not look like what I've been through. Yet I am tired of holding it in. So, damn what they say, I am standing on the promises of what God said. *The promises of the Lord are yes and Amen* (2 Corinthians 1:20). So, if it means that I have to open my house of horrors so all can see, then be my guest. You too are welcome to explore, open the drawers, cabinets, and closet doors. Walk through and stay as long as you would like. I invite you to see me naked and unashamed because I am who God has made me to be. I am Christine Renee, Christian Reborn. I am not who I used to be, by the grace of Jesus Christ (Yahshua), I have been set free. I would like to extend an open invitation for you to join me.

Lamentations 3 (22-27) gives me hope that the scars of the past were simply my transportation vehicle to the serene peace I've found in the arms of the Lord. It's my profound wish that every one of you reading this book would find your way to this place as well by acknowledging Jesus Christ as your personal Lord and Savior. With an invitation to come in and stay a while, long enough for change and complete healing to settle into your souls. Long enough for the chains of slavery to fall off.

It is not as unattainable as you may imagine. It is as simple as saying a few words with heartfelt meaning. These few words can be spoken in any situation or circumstance or wherever you find yourself standing at this moment. No matter how bad you think it is. God can come in right where you are if invited. We must remember that the power behind our prayer is passion. James 5 (15-16) gives us an introduction to the prayer of faith and instructions on how to achieve success.

Dear God in heaven, I come to you in the name of Jesus. I acknowledge to you that I am a sinner, and I am sorry for my sins and the life that I have lived; I need your forgiveness. I believe that your only begotten Son Jesus Christ shed his precious blood on the cross at Calvary and died for my sins, and I am now willing to turn from my sin. You said in the bible that if we confess to the Lord our God and believe in our hearts that God raised Jesus from the dead, we shall be saved. Right now, I confess to Jesus as my Lord. With my heart, I believe that God raised Jesus from the dead. This very moment I accept Jesus Christ as my own personal Savior and according to his Word, right now I am saved. Amen. (paulbarksdale.com)

The power of life and death (Proverbs 18:21) is our free will to speak into existence what we honestly believe. This was the season where I learned to rehearse the promises of God. I wanted to speak life.

The healing process takes on the challenge of pain. It goes through the agony of discomfort. Before it ever sees the light of day that ushers in healing. It is overbearing, ten toes down, as you give into the pain of pushing yourself to find relief. Ask any mother about the natural process of childbirth and they will depict a picture of pure bliss that at first, seemed like near death. Breaking free is like giving birth. You open up to the pain to find the miracle that awaits you on the other side. There is no way around it, no matter what they say, we can never forget what God said nor his promises for us.

We have the free will to change our point of view. By changing our perspective, we allow the opportunity for grace to operate at its full potential. Our frame of reference is not always what is needed at the time. When we are trusting God, we are allowing everything outside of ourselves to happen as they should while we stand on his promises. We should remember it's never what it seems. The frustration, the loss, the mistakes neither are what they appear to be but instead, it's all a part of the greater plan for our lives. These things only come to determine which path will lead to the destination that is already designed for us. It is up to us to choose to grant grace to ourselves and others during times when it's most difficult. The application of grace allows our perspective to evolve and transform our lives all together.

If Jesus had not granted us grace, where would any of us be today? It is the sweet loveliness that he had for us as sinners before we were even born that has allowed us to be free today. The smell of grace is sweet and inviting. It has no boundaries and it seeps in, finding itself within the confined places, opening areas long forgotten. There isn't anything left untouched. When the Savior saves, he brings forth total and complete healing from ourselves which at first, seems like nothing but once it's truly revealed, it can be defined as nothing but grace.

www.ingramcontent.com/pod-product-compliance
Lightning Source LLC
Chambersburg PA
CBHW070041100426
42740CB00013B/2754